FAMILY INSIGHTS
through the
SHORT STORY

by
Rose M. Somerville

HUMAN RELATIONS AND THE FAMILY
Paul Vahanian, Editor

Born out of widespread concern for the growing symptoms of individual and family instability, this series focuses on the role of education in combating and preventing further deterioration in family relationships. It is hoped that teachers, school administrators and others will discover in this series suggestions for helping learners respond more effectively to the challenges of modern society.

FAMILY
INSIGHTS
through the
SHORT STORY

A Guide for
Teachers and Workshop Leaders

Rose M. Somerville

Bureau of Publications
Teachers College, Columbia University
New York • 1964

Cover design by Donn Devita

Introduction

In *Family Insights Through the Short Story,* Rose Somerville offers a creative design for teaching and studying family life through the use of imaginative literature. By focussing on significant themes in family living, Dr. Somerville illustrates how the short story can be employed to facilitate growth in understanding of human relationships.

Dr. Somerville began this project during a year of intern teaching at Teachers College, Columbia University, with the late Professor Ernest Osborne. She has spent many years reading and testing stories in a diversity of classrooms and workshops, including The New School for Social Research, Brooklyn College, Hunter College, and the Roosevelt Hospital School of Nursing. A pioneering effort, *Family Insights Through the Short Story* fills a notable gap in the field, and does so with economy, with clarity, and with sensitive appreciation of the many issues in family relationships that can benefit by illumination through the humanities.

The book is divided into two parts. In the first part the reader will find a general orientation about the uses of fiction in teaching, the selection and acquisition of short stories, and the ways of using stories. The second part includes ten chapters devoted to the major content areas of family study: the changing roles of men and women, adolescents and young adults, dating and mate selection, sex standards, the unmarried adult, marital adjustment, parent-child and sibling relationships, family disorganization, aging and the aged, and bereavement. Each of these chapters includes a comprehensive list of pertinent stories, plus two or three full story summaries. These summaries are in turn accompanied by suggested themes for discussion.

v

For most readers the appendices will prove of considerable additional value. These include, in Appendix A, a bibliography of related readings; in Appendix B, a master list of over a hundred stories; and, in Appendix C, a comprehensive index of problem areas covered in the master list of stories.

PAUL VAHANIAN

Contents

FAMILY
INSIGHTS
through the
SHORT STORY

PART I

LITERATURE AND THE STUDY
OF THE FAMILY

1

The Use of Fiction in Teaching the Social Sciences

INTERDISCIPLINARY POTENTIALS

Since the inception of family life education, an interdisciplinary approach has been evident. Courses in marriage and the family have for several decades turned to such disciplines as psychology, sociology, economics, and history for what they could contribute to family study in methodology and in data. Now, a reciprocal trend seems to be developing. In the past decade educators have been taking increased cognizance of the contributions that family life education can make to their disciplines.[1]

There is room, however, for further interdisciplinary enrichment. The humanities have been largely neglected as a source of insight into the family as process and as institution. Yet with the educational goals of family life education, and its marked humanistic orientation, it could hardly find a more appropriate resource than that of imaginative literature, whether in the form of novels, plays, poems, or short stories. The family life educator seeks to aid the student in understanding himself as a family member in a given society and thereby to increase his comprehension of general behavioral principles and of social institutions. Literature has much to offer toward these ends. It not only provides revelations of motivations of human behavior in a diversity of cultures but it tends to bring to the fore controversial issues of private practice and public policy.

[1]See, for example, William E. Hall, *Family Life Education—An Opportunity for Psychological Instruction;* M. Eunice Hilton, *The Guidance Worker and Family Life Education;* and Clifford F. S. Bebell, *Family Life Education Contributes to the Preparation of Teachers,* as well as other pamphlets in the series developed by the Middle States Project on Education for Personal and Family Living, American Social Health Association, 1790 Broadway, New York, N.Y. 10019.

PRECEDENTS AND MODELS

Any explanation of the relative slowness in turning to fiction for an illumination of family relationships will have to take into account the family life educator's lack of familiarity with modern literature and with the approach to creative work which emphasizes the human relations rather than the esthetic aspects.

In this respect his colleagues in other fields—especially in psychology and indeed in departments of literature—have been more fortunate. Literature teachers have pioneered in the human relations emphasis not only in the classroom but in elaborating the theoretical basis of the interdependence of fiction and the social sciences. Psychology teachers have seen the possibility of progressing from case materials to the assignment of novels and plays. They have reported in the professional journals on the positive results of introducing fiction into the psychology classroom. On the clinical level, psychotherapists and librarians have been cooperating to found a new field: *bibliotherapy*. The ancient conception of books as "medicine for the soul" has been extended to the treatment of mental illness, with patients being helped to work through to the real world by way of the fictional.

Encouraging as these precedents are in suggesting the potentialities of literature for increasing psychological and sociological awareness, they offer little in the way of models to the family life educator. Because of their heavy reliance on novels and their lack of specific focus on the family, it is necessary for the many educators who deal with family study to look elsewhere for practical aid.

THE SHORT-STORY RESOURCE

The advantages of shorter forms of fiction are particularly marked for family life education. It is necessary in family study to examine many facets of relationship in many phases of the life cycle. The short story meets this need for diversity of assignment. Family study stresses classroom discussion. The short story allows teacher and students to gain sufficient grasp of the details of the family interrelationship to discuss them without searching for "page and verse."

The short story resource is useful to all educators who deal with family relationships. This includes, above all, the teacher in family courses, whether in sociology, home economics, or human relations departments. But it is not only family courses as such that deal with family subject matter. There are literature courses that include family units; education courses that direct the attention of future teachers to the home-school relationship and the problems of knowing the family backgrounds of students and of handling parent-teacher conferences; child development and adolescence courses, whether offered in psychology, education, or other departments of a college; courses in schools of nursing that prepare nurses to work with patients of diverse family subcultures; guidance courses that prepare homeroom teachers and counselors to recognize the family roots of school behaviors; the many courses in ethics, social philosophy, comparative government, and social problems which explore changing norms and role allocations through the centuries and in given societies.

The short story is useful not only to teachers in a school setting but to the many leaders, lay and professional, who are responsible for single-meeting and continuing discussion groups in a variety of other settings. The short story provides for workshop participants a common stimulus that can be particularly helpful in situations in which (1) there is uneven academic background and (2) emotion-laden aspects of interpersonal relationships will be explored without prior opportunity to develop the group unity and trust prerequisite to free discussion. Therefore, the short-story resource can be of aid in community workshops concerned with mental health, social hygiene, or public affairs, as well as in the diverse adult education courses offered in a variety of institutional settings: parent institutes, church study circles, club activities of the "Y" type, and guidance-clinic classes.

WHY FICTION IS EFFECTIVE IN FAMILY STUDY

There are several theoretical bases for the effectiveness of fiction in functional teaching.

1. Research in empathy finds a high degree of correlation between self-understanding and the ability to understand others. The student who develops an awareness of his own feelings, behaviors, and goals as a family member can better understand these phenomena in others. Fiction draws him into imaginary participation in family situations and interaction. He shares the feelings of the character with whom he identifies and thereby becomes alert to the motivations of other characters in the story.

Classroom analysis of the story offers the student an opportunity to compare with his classmates the inferences he has made concerning affect and intent of characters and the conclusions he has drawn concerning social pressures operative in the situation. Disparities in the analysis of story behaviors, when seen to rest on different value orientations and social norm interpretations as well as degree of perceptive skill, move the student to clarify his thoughts and attitudes about family relationships.

2. The blending of the emotional and the rational in fiction provides the reader with dual satisfactions. The tragic story has both cathartic and stimulating effects. Emotions previously repressed are permitted expression. Intellectual curiosity about the relation of man to society is given evidence to weigh.

From the story experience the student learns to accept emotion and to cope with feeling-laden situations rationally. By arousing his emotions, fiction offers the student the lifelike context in which alternatives have to be delimited and decisions made in matters that concern the family. Moreover, by enhancing the feeling of personal involvement and significance that is basic to human growth, fiction tends to assure further learnings by the student. Imaginative literature becomes a lifetime resource for the continued study of self and society, which modern family adjustment requires.

3. Fiction provides vicarious experiences in a great variety of family settings and situations. Thus the student is exposed to family interaction rarely accessible to firsthand observation. Religious, socioeconomic, or racial lines drawn in the larger society or in the community ordinarily limit the student's range of understanding. Fiction can partly erase these lines and make available for study the structure and functioning of a number of family subcultures.

Moreover, it is only through the vicarious experience offered by fiction that the student who has been sheltered from family experiences of a painful sort can achieve understanding of family crises such as divorce, illness, or bereavement. Feeling the impact of such situations on family members, the student is motivated thoughtfully to analyze the destructive interaction and seek out preventive and corrective elements. He becomes an actor rather than an onlooker in social problems, concerned as individual and as citizen to find solutions rather than sit in judgment.

4. The student learns to distinguish between the individual instance and the broad generalization when he is aided in the classroom to relate the idiosyncratic story to the behavioral principles and sociological findings presented in text and reference readings. Fiction reinforces learnings about the family derived from other sources and serves to illustrate their complexity.

HOW FICTION FACILITATES ROLE PERFORMANCE BY TEACHER AND STUDENT

The norms of teacher and student responsibility are changing. Fiction can help in several ways to encourage fulfillment of new expectations.

1. The student is asked to participate actively in discussion in order to derive maximum benefit from attending classes. However, the heritage of the traditional lecture situation has created a problem in this regard: the student tends to sit passively and await the teacher's pronouncements. The teacher is hesitant to exercise pressure or coercion for oral expression of student ideas lest the values of self-motivated communication be undermined. Fiction helps them avoid this impasse. Because stories are exciting and because the student tends to identify himself with a fictional character, he is likely to lose self-consciousness and enjoy the opportunity to contribute to the group discussion. Moreover, since the focus is on the fictional characters, the student can cloak his own concerns and without fear of exposure enter into the discussion of personal and social problems that are significant to him.

2. To teach students or to teach subject matter is no longer an alternative of polarities when subject matter in the classroom is geared to the life tasks of the student. The teacher must offer reading materials of considerable breadth if the course is to meet the needs of students, for these needs are diverse even within a narrow age group. Fiction helps to create relevance of classroom education to dissimilar task urgencies. In the stories there are characters who face life tasks of varying kind and proportion. Those students who are finding occupational choice the strongest current challenge will seek out what the story offers in this regard while the same story will allow those concerned with sex impulses to concentrate on decision-making and consequences in this area. Considerations of student readiness are more easily taken into account when at least some of the course readings permit the student to find his own level on which to maximize learnings.

Relatedly, the guidance role of the teacher can be more sensitively fulfilled when stories are part of the course work. The response of the student to fictional events often reveals his level of knowledge and the range of his interests, his confusions, and his aspirations. Because the student has been freed to participate more readily, as risk has been reduced by objectification of the problem, he offers the teacher more evidence on which to determine meaningful assignments for him, whether additional readings or new experiences through field work.

3. The student's reading assignments, markedly increased with the "knowledge explosion" of the present decade, include many formidable texts. Fiction heightens the pleasurable aspects of study, providing a counterweight to the more difficult abstractions and increasing confidence in ability to master course content. The enjoyment of a course has positive effects upon study motivation. But unlike the sugar-coating of a bitter pill, stories of high literary quality are in themselves an enriching experience. Moreover, they are a bridge to other human beings: to fellow students, to parents, teachers, friends—the "significant others." Students report that stories have encouraged exploration in the home and in the dormitory of vital aspects of personal relationship and social structure rarely attempted before. These "others" constitute an unregistered student body beyond the circle of class members. Unlike study which curtails contacts with friends and family, this sharing of experience links up meaningfully various facets of a student's existence. For engaged students a joint examination of stories may permit the kind of exploration of feelings, attitudes, and values frequently urged as an indispensable prelude to marriage commitment.

SUMMARY

Family study has long been interdisciplinary. Cross-fertilization with imaginative literature, however, has been one-sided so far, with literature teachers rather than family life educators realizing the potential of using fiction for human relations insights. Psychologists and bibliotherapists have made use of the literature resource but their concentration on novels and plays offers little practical precedent. The family life educator needs a literary form which will allow many facets of family relationship to be explored. The short story offers this diversity of theme as well as the brevity that facilitates classroom discussion. In and out of academic settings, the short story provides a common experience that encourages student interaction and overcomes educational and emotional barriers to joint problem-solving.

Fiction's utility in family study finds theoretical explanation in the self-other findings of empathy research, the emotional-rational components of decision making in life situations, and vicarious experience as one of the multiple sources of knowledge about self and the social process.

Student-teacher complementarity in the modern classroom is aided by the stimulus of fiction, with the student more easily fitting into an active role and the teacher gaining from student activity increased insights into further growth needs. The relevance of class activity for the student's task urgencies is enhanced by the differential focus each story permits. And the sense of mastery which fiction offers the student builds enjoyment in study and encourages a union of the worlds inside and outside the classroom into a meaningful whole.

2

Selecting and Obtaining
Copies of Short Stories

CRITERIA

The abundance of short stories containing family themes permits the teacher to set at least three basic criteria for selection. These are style, setting, and insight, all of which are relevant to the objectives of using fiction in studying the family.

1. The *style* of writing can facilitate or hamper the student's ability to experience the events as though they were occurring to him personally (identification) or to put himself into the emotional framework of others (empathy). To many students, the literary classics do not communicate intelligibly—let alone movingly. This is unfortunate, but it is perhaps foolhardy for the educator using fiction in family study to attempt singlehandedly to change student attitudes toward literature that have been years in the making. He is already presenting the student with enough deviations from expected procedure by introducing fiction into the social science course, using the short story instead of the usual novel or play, and permitting a broad range of interpretation. He should not add to these multiple challenges. Naturally, when the teacher has evidence that a particular class is exceptional, that it can identify easily with Jason or Medea, Lear or Cordelia, Natasha or Andrey, then the centuries of literature are at his disposal. However, the average class will gain more if the teacher is content to cut the fictional thread at the turn of the century and choose stories with a modern style.

2. Diversity of *setting* is another criterion in story selection. To develop alertness to stereotypes, to gain awareness of the many subcultures in a society, to make cross-cultural comparisons, the student must be acquainted with the various designs for family living in different societies and among different socioeconomic groups. Trans-

lations of foreign literature are a helpful supplement to stories by American writers, who may tend to a preoccupation with the urban, middle-class family.

3. Perhaps the most important criterion of all is the degree of psychological and social *insight* revealed by the story writer, his informed sensitivity to the feelings of family members and to the texture of the social fabric in which the family institution is wrapped. The story is most useful when it illuminates the social process in such a way that the student can acquire "evidence" for the inferences he makes concerning the meaning of the behaviors depicted, when clues to motives and feelings can be found by careful reading.

SOURCES

Faced with making a choice among the formidable array of short stories available to him, the family life educator can find little bibliographic aid in standard sources. Despite the publication in recent decades of short stories that compare favorably with other fiction in terms of literary quality, the tradition of the novel is still so strong as to create a marked lag in the classification and annotation of short stories in reference works. Even in the major bibliographic sources, shorter works of fiction are either not provided with subject categories or are grouped together for classification. If a given anthology is described as "tales of misery and despair," the educator cannot know without first reading the entire volume which story focuses upon which source of misery and despair, which family relationship, and which family subculture.

The most helpful source in the selection of stories is the *Short Story Index*. Almost a hundred of its subject headings are obviously family-related, ranging from adolescence, adoption, and adultery to wife-beating, woman, and youth. The first volume catalogs sixty thousand stories in collections published before 1949, and the two supplementary volumes add almost sixteen thousand more, published through 1958. A fourth volume will cover stories from 1959 to 1963. Under each subject heading authors are listed alphabetically, with titles of their stories and the anthologies in which they appear.

However, even with the aid of the *Short Story Index* there remains a considerable burden of research to find stories appropriate to class work. The *Index* is more helpful after the teacher has formed some opinions about authors and anthology series most helpful to family study. Part II of the present book, is intended as an introductory bibliographical tool for the teacher. From the specific stories suggested he will learn the names of effective writers, the best story collections available, and various editors and publishers in the short-story field.

It will be evident that few stories in the mass-media publications meet the criteria established. More serious, perhaps, than their lack of literary merit is their limited scope in defining alternative choices that face family members, feelings that fall within the range of the normal, and problems that actually concern family members in various social settings. Most of the stories selected in Part II have come from anthologies which periodically bring together the best of the stories that have appeared first in obscure literary journals. The "tight" literary form of the short story, which makes it so economical of classroom time, constitutes a challenge to creative writers. Many noted novelists have tried their hand at shorter fiction without overwhelming success. In choosing stories, the educator should try to be receptive to the work of lesser-known writers, placing more importance on the story's family insights than its place in the history of literature.

The fund of diverse stories described in Part II represents this kind of selection. Each story has been used in the classroom and found, by analysis of discussion tapes, to be effective in family study. The teacher who starts with these stories, selecting from among them those that seem most suitable to his classes, can acquire experience in the use of literature before embarking on the enjoyable but time-consuming search for new stories. To provide some help in that search, Part II also offers a "Reserve" listing, giving titles of stories that have been successfully used in teaching situations but providing no detailed description. This may be particularly welcomed by the teacher who is impatient of others' concepts of *the* key problems in a story; by using the Reserve list only, he can readily put his hand on relevant stories and work out his own understandings.

OBTAINING COPIES OF STORIES FOR STUDENT USE

The decision to use a story will in part rest on its availability. Most of the stories listed in Part II appear in paperback form, some in hardcover as well, only a few in hardcover only. Even when the teacher has good library facilities, it is well to consult in advance and secure cooperation in getting paperbacks bound before they are placed on reserve shelves. If the teacher wishes each student to have a copy of the story, it is necessary for the local bookstore or the teacher himself to contact the publisher directly, allowing three to four weeks for delivery from distant points.

While many paperbacks not on view in bookstores are obtainable from the publishers, many others will be in short supply or out of print. However, for such stories permission is often granted the teacher or the institution to mimeograph or otherwise reproduce the story for class use. This is not cheap, however. It is advisable for the teacher to use the story, in its library copy form, with several classes before deciding that this is a story he will want to use and re-use and therefore worth the costs of reproduction. It is aso desirable to check with the author or other copyright holder or in any event to consult the latest volume of *Short Story Index* to see whether the given story has since been selected for inclusion in another anthology.

3

Ways of
Using Stories

ASSIGNING STORIES

There are stories available for each part of the course work. However, how many stories a teacher should use in a course will depend on a great many factors that vary in each institution and each class: whether the course meets for one or for two semesters, whether the teacher is experienced in working with fiction, whether the desired stories are easily available in the library, through purchase, or through reproduction, whether films, role-playing, panel reports, and field trips are already consuming a considerable part of class time, and whether the atmosphere is conducive to extensive experimentation with the new stimulus.

Whatever the decision as to number, which may vary from one or two to one or two dozen, the question will arise as to when to assign the stories. The teacher has three choices: to assign all stories at the beginning of the term, to assign one or two at a time as the course proceeds, or to assign most at the beginning and add stories ocasionally. Each method has its advantages and its difficulties.

If all the stories are assigned at the beginning, each can be listed in the course outline or syllabus, along with the textbooks and reference readings, under the topics to be covered during the term. This gives the story equal status as course material and moreover helps to clarify what the story is intended to illuminate, thereby minimizing inquiry as to "what to look for when reading the story." A general instruction can be given to focus on *"who in the story is doing what, to whom, and why."* The difficulty with early selection of the stories and their incorporation into the course outline is that flexibility of assignment is lost. The class may move in unexpected directions, since its needs and make-up can only generally be anticipated. The relevancy of a story for the particular class may be diminished by the time the assignment is due. Also, the use of a newly discovered story must be deferred until the next course outline is drawn up instead of using it when the teacher's own enthusiasm and interest are at a peak.

Assigning stories one or two at a time throughout the semester has the virtue of flexibility but the drawback of the unexpected. The student may interpret the new assignment as "extra" work and resent an addition to a busy study schedule, or may regard it as less significant a learning vehicle than the basic readings assigned initially.

If most of the stories are assigned at the beginning and the students prepared for the additions that may come later, the advantages of flexibility and stability are both likely to be gained.

It should be noted, however, that the disadvantages attaching to the first two choices can be mitigated in a number of ways. Because most stories have several themes, the problem of relevancy is rarely an acute one; a skillful discussion leader can help the group to focus on the aspect of the story that has the most pertinence for the given moment. Also, the teacher's enthusiasm for a newfound story can be reawakened for its deferred use by a fresh reading. If this fails to come about, the delay may have been fortunate for it will have led to a necessary modification in the original estimate of the story's potential. And, finally, student attitudes toward the introduction of new reading assignments during the term's work can be favorably affected by the kinds of statement made by the teacher in the class and in the course outline, particularly if the addition of text and reference readings is already a normal procedure.

Perhaps the most decisive argument for an assignment schedule that retains some degree of flexibility is the fact that only to that extent will the teacher be able to take advantage of the following five purposes which can be served by introducing a story as the course develops:

A change of pace. A story can slow down or speed up the tempo of class discussion, with positive effects on alertness and interest.

A common experience. A story can unite class members, especially when diverse academic or personal backgrounds make it difficult for them to relate to one another.

A supplement. A story can provide additional information in areas where textbook and reference materials are inadequate or outdated.

A provocation. A story can facilitate exploration of subject matter not readily talked about; the author's willingness to face problematical issues openly allows the student to bring forth hidden attitudes.

A correction. A story can reveal to the class the biases they have been expressing. Student views are more open to modification when awareness is developed through comment on story characters and defensive needs are at a minimum.

INTEGRATING STORIES INTO ONGOING COURSES

Whatever the number and timing of story assignments, there are several ways in which stories can be used in an established course: as the focus of class discussion, the subject of a report by a student panel, the theme of book reviews, logs, or papers, or the basis for examination questions.

For all these, class discussion of the first story selected by the teacher is essential. Even if subsequent stories will not be discussed in class (either because time will not permit, or because a large class cannot conveniently be broken up into discussion groups of fifteen or so with any regularity), it is desirable to make provision for a detailed analysis of the first story. This discussion will establish the norms for story reading and interpretation. Even a single experience of small group exploration of the family insights in the story will affect later story reading positively, for the student will carry over some degree of awareness of the diverse contributions that class members offer. He will also have gained the essential impression that the teacher expected him to adduce "evidence," clues provided by the author, for any assertions concerning motivations of the characters. In a course that emphasizes the social context of family development, the teacher's questions concerning roles, institutions, and mores will have directed the student's attention to this dimension of story analysis. In a course that emphasizes personal development, the teacher's questions concerning interaction among the story characters will have shown the student that perceptive skill was a central consideration.

If the story is a complex one, and this is usually the desirable choice for an initial story as the student will be receiving maximum help from teacher and classmates, the teacher can encourage the class to divide the story into units of analysis that are most natural to the situation depicted. In one story this may be the unit of relationship: father–daughter, boy–grandfather, or any other dyadic combination. In another story it may be by points of time: the relationships among the family members before the crisis and after. In still another, it may be the extra-family contacts of each member. It is important for the class to see that there is no fixed pattern to be applied to all stories and that for any one story there may be a choice of ways in which to establish units of analysis. A simple story may not require any discussion structure at all, as all the relationships may be understood simultaneously.

The alternative to a model group discussion of a story as an initial literature experience in the course is the use of guide questions supplied the students by the teacher. In such questions the teacher points the attention of the class in specific directions. This has the danger of reducing the emotional impact of the story. Even if carefully instructed to read a story twice, first for the emotional experience and only the second time pausing for analysis, the student can be limited by a framework of specific questions. The opportunity to respond creatively to the story, to formulate his own questions, is reduced. Class discussion with students who have depended on the teacher's guide questions is often formal and limited. Without class discussion the student's reliance on the guide questions tends to be even further increased. It should be noted that the problem of guide questions is not peculiar to fiction but arises in connection with films and indeed with textbook materials. In this matter the teacher must make his own decision. If he uses guide questions in other areas of the course, he will probably be more comfortable in offering these for stories as well.

For stories assigned after the initial one, if class discussion is not possible, it is desirable to encourage informal interchange among the students in out-of-class gatherings. This can sometimes combine well with student panel reports. Such reports in the classroom are less time-consuming than discussion by the whole class and often pinpoint areas of disagreement that can be further explored in dormitories and at lunch tables. If student interest in a particular story is high, the teacher can encourage some feedback from the informal encounters during the class session.

Written work is preferably a supplement to rather than a substitute for class discussion. However, where class time is not available, analysis of a story can take written form. This helps the student formulate his ideas about the story and provides the teacher with clues to his development. It must be recognized that it does not permit the student to benefit from interchange with his classmates. To make this possible, the students can be divided up into four- or five-member committees, each of which meets out of class to discuss the story and write a joint report.

Whether or not the story has been examined in class, it can be included in mid-term and end-term examinations to test student insight and comprehension. If several stories have been used during the term, the examination question can ask the student to relate one to the other, offering comparisons and contrasts. Or the student can be asked to use the stories he has read to illustrate his answers to questions based on other materials in the course.

The integration of the story into the ongoing course should be regarded as an enrichment of, and not a substitute for other media of student involvement. Stories and films used in the course can be compared in terms of specific variables in the situations depicted and the kinds of outcomes. Stories can give impetus to role-playing in which the effects of personal interaction are experienced. Field trips can be organized on the basis of interest aroused by stories in family courts, child care institutions, project housing, ethnic sections of the community, and counseling centers.

Teachers differ in their ease of handling the various resources available for classroom effectiveness. Skill in the use of fiction comes relatively quickly, however, even with a cautious introduction of one or two stories into a course. Literature appetite grows by what it feeds on and the new enthusiast may have to be careful to limit his story assignments to maintain balance of materials. Full use of the short story can be achieved only in a special course.

DEVELOPING A NEW COURSE OF FAMILY STUDY

Stories may serve as the basis for a new course. Emphasis here will be given to a new family course, although comparable possibilities exist for new courses in child development, adolescence, and social problems.

In the new course the stories constitute the main readings, with textbook and reference materials as supplementary assignments. If the class has had little work in psychology and sociology, particularly child and adolescent psychology and social stratification, it is desirable to coordinate readings of this kind with the story assignments. If the class is academically advanced, the supplementary readings may be largely from professional journals which report current research. In adult education courses, the teacher can reduce the amount of required reading while providing needed background knowledge by distributing mimeographed selections from basic writings in a given area or by summarizing pertinent passages. In many instances separate discussion of such materials is not necessary because the students will be bringing into the story discussion whatever of the didactic readings has had significance for them.

Course Design

The new course has several alternative sequences. The major content areas of family study may be examined in the order in which they are arranged in Part II, or they may start at some other point in the life cycle of an individual or of a family. There are a number of logical sequences that are equally defensible. There is a certain amount of overlapping among the topics, but these can be treated as points of re-emphasis.

If the course follows the pattern of the individual life cycle, stories that focus first of all on the coming of the baby will be selected, followed by the relation of the young child to parents, siblings, and peer group; the adolescent and his developmental tasks; the young adult and his family of procreation; the middle years that bring to a new level the problems of in-laws, finances, life goals, and relationships with children and with parents; the "empty nest" with its re-establishment of dyadic interaction; old age and role reversals; and, finally, the impact of bereavement on surviving family members.

If the course follows the family cycle, it may spin the wheel first of all to the point of origin of the nuclear family, examining courtship and the roles of men and women in a changing society; continuing with the young couple and their adjustments to each other, to their in-laws, and to the coming of children; the middle-aged couple with their adolescent children and aging parents; the elderly couple and then the lone survivor; and throughout all these stages the various crises, such as illness, unemployment, separation, desertion, and divorce, that may interrupt the family cycle at any point, leaving fragmented and vestigial families to fulfill primary group functions.

In any course design there will be a great variety of subthemes that can be explored, such as family planning, abortion, illegitimacy, adoption, sex deviancy, and infidelity, as well as ceremony, religion, budgets, family counseling, and community relationships. Because these fit under a number of themes in the life cycle course design, the teacher will have to decide at what point in the course to examine them and their relative importance to the course. The decision will depend on the purposes of the course and the composition of the student body in terms of age, task urgencies, and interests. The duration of the course and its relationship to other parts of the curriculum are additional factors in the problem of completeness.

The discussion themes suggested for each story described in Part II are appropriate in any course design adopted, and allow for a wide variation of themes and subthemes included in various courses. By making clear in the story assignment which family theme it is intended to illuminate, the teacher can help the class to focus on the aspect that is most relevant, reserving for other parts of the course reference to other themes in the story. Thus it is possible to use "A Country Weekend" for a discussion of the working wife and mother and to reserve for another occasion consideration of premarital sex relationships and infidelity. It may be impossible to avoid reference to some of the other themes when a story is under discussion, but the class can be assured that a fuller exploration of them will be undertaken at a later point.

The age of the student group is a significant factor in designing the course. The college student is usually concerned with problems of dating and courtship and may be more likely to respond to a course which begins with these or with the related topic of masculine and feminine roles. He may have little interest in childhood problems until he sees them in relation to himself as parent. Then his ideas of child-rearing will make the question of the rearing he has received seem highly relevant. Similarly, an interest in the middle years of marriage and in aging may develop only as he sees a personal relevance to his current problems of mate selection and relationships to parents and future in-laws.

A middle-aged class or one in which older students predominate (typical in adult education, especially in communities where women resume their education when children enter school) tends to respond well to a course sequence that begins with marriage in the middle years, where interest centers on role changes and relationships with adolescent children and aging parents. Interest in dating and mate selection, sex standards, and family planning develops through the pertinence of these themes for their family members.

Whatever the design of the course, it must devote its initial meeting to an orientation session.

Orientation Session

The course that places its main reliance on the psychosocial insights of fiction requires an orientation session to clarify expectations, both as to goals and as to procedures. Student participation can be invited in these formulations but it is the teacher's responsibility to make sure that the main points receive emphasis and elaboration. A brief story read aloud in class by the students in rotation helps to concretize these points. The teacher will ordinarily have to bring sufficient copies of the story to class as the students will not yet have acquired their reading lists. But the results usually repay this effort. Not only is a working model established of classroom procedures but the students are from the first placed in an active role in the course work. The alternative, a lecture by the teacher, may create expectations of student-teacher relationship that will have to be corrected in subsequent meetings. The following require emphasis in the orientation session:

1. The human relationships revealed by the story, rather than literary aspects, will be the class focus. How the writer achieves his effects, whether the story is in his usual style, how his own life has led him to certain preoccupations, his stature in literary criticism—these and related questions are outside the scope of the family course. One might perhaps say that for the purposes of this class the story has no author at all. It will not be unexpected, however, if the student has enjoyed a story by a given author that he may be motivated to look for further writings of his.

The teacher can help the students to focus on the story rather than the author by referring always to the story title, as, for example, "Do you recall when we were reading 'None Sing So Wildly' . . .," rather than "In that story by James Jones we discussed a few weeks ago. . . ." Such references should be handled with particular care in the orientation session.

2. The stories will be by a variety of authors, some known and some unknown. Famous writers do not always provide the best short stories on family themes. Stories have been selected for their psychological and social insights. Sometimes a writer whose name is associated with the shallow and the banal will have a story that is highly perceptive. A fresh approach to each story, avoiding preconceptions, will ensure the response it deserves.

The teacher can help the students handle the connotations that attach to the names of some writers by articulating some of their feelings, as, for example, "Many of us think of Edna Ferber as one who. . . ."

3. The stories are selected mainly from paperback collections. This is not only for purposes of economy, but also to tap sources of new and experimental writing. To ensure the wide distribution that paperback fiction requires to pay for itself, some publishers use sensational pictures on their book covers; therefore, paperbacks are not to be judged by their covers, no matter how lurid; there is a course-worth of difference between a "whodunnit" and a "whydunnit." The student may occasionally have to explain this difference to friends and relatives.

The teacher perhaps more rarely will have a similar public relations job to do with librarians whose attitudes to paperback fiction are happily now in process of change. Many of the stories described in Part II are also available in hardback editions and these should be ordered for the library wherever possible.

4. Each story requires at least two readings. In the first reading the student allows himself to experience the emotions aroused by it and to react spontaneously to the situation and the characters. In the second reading, preferably separated in time, the student will begin to analyze the behaviors of the story characters, noting behavioral clues to motivation and emotion and taking specific cognizance of the social pressures operative in the situation.

At each class meeting the teacher can remind the students of this expectation by asking how many felt it necessary to read the particular story more than twice.

5. While not ordinarily inquired into in the classroom, the student interested in understanding himself as a family member will note with which characters he identified, which he disliked, and why. He may find, after several stories, that his attitudes fall into a pattern he was not fully aware of. He may accept this or wish to change it.

The teacher can bring this matter of identification to the fore by inquiring occasionally whether any student had identified with this or that character.

6. The stories are not cheerful as a rule, but emotional satisfaction sometimes derives from their cathartic effects. Moreover, the destructive interaction depicted motivates the student to analyze causal factors and search for solutions other than those attempted by the fictional characters.

The teacher can help the students acknowledge their emotions and recognize the feeling component in decision-making.

7. Since group discussion places maximum reliance on the student's own critical thinking and frank expression of this thought, the group has some degree of responsibility in cooperating with the teacher to create a warm and accepting classroom climate. In their efforts to learn from one another they will be aided by the nature of the experience: the commonality of the focus, the humanistic goal, the variety of human aspirations and fears revealed, and the fundamental interdependence of needs that emerges.

The Teacher's Role as Discussion Leader

A new family course based on the insights of literature presumes a teacher who regards the student's active participation as prerequisite to intellectual growth and attitudinal change. This teacher recognizes that what the student has to contribute, however unpolished in formulation, is of value in his effort to work through to his own insights. Unlike the family course in which some balance is usually attempted between lecturing and class discussion, the new course approaches its goals largely through the latter. The teacher has three special responsibilities in this regard:

Encouraging student participation. This involves not only positive efforts on the teacher's part but significant restraints. Immediate and sharp correction of a student's contribution is avoided. If another student has not questioned the statement, the teacher may relate it to a previous question, offer a modified formulation, and ask the student if he would accept this. Or the teacher may let the statement go without comment and return to it in another context, which may be less threatening to the student who needs special encouragemen to venture his views. Furthermore, the teacher serves as a model in his willingness to listen attentively, without interrupting.

Offering help to the group. Consonant with the effort not to impair student initiative or to force discussion into predetermined channels, the teacher can provide structure and can aid in keeping the discussion in focus. He can bring the students back from a digression which is not proving fruitful to them. He can encourage the students to depart from the story's limits and consider the effects of changing one factor: as, for example, when a son rather than a daughter challenges the parent; an older woman rather than a young one is deserted by her husband.

Becoming a group member himself. By planning the room arrangement, the teacher can avoid a status placement for himself. A seminar table or circular seating enables the class members to see one another and permits the teacher to merge with the group, thereby increasing the likelihood of student-student interaction. The teacher may find he has to learn to rely less on notes and prepared materials when these no longer have the shelter of a desk. This requires more careful preparation in advance. It also serves to hold his contributions in check. Literature may be unique in the degree to which it reminds the teacher of his followership functions in group discussion; probably in few other teaching situations does he find his students contributing so much to his own insights and awarenesses.

Preparatory and Follow-up Experiences

Illustrative material posted around the room can be prepared by a student committee. Clippings from newspapers and magazines that relate to the theme of the story under discussion may be asked of each student. This is not merely a device to create a dramatic atmosphere, although the visual stimulus of colorful pictures is not to be discounted, but it serves to reveal the contrasting levels on which the mass media and academic sources handle the same family problems. The pressures of the culture become factors to reckon with in the classroom.

Buzz groups may be formed preparatory to discussion by the whole class. In these small groups of three, four, or five students, some preliminary examination of the story can take place, with a reporter from each buzz group bringing to the class points of agreement and disagreement arrived at on a conversational level.

Occasionally before class discussion begins, the students may be asked to react to a story in writing. This often serves to heighten the student's awareness of what he gains from the group's analysis. It also provides the teacher with a better estimate of the abilities of a student whose class participation is uneven. The written report can serve as the basis of a teacher-student conference or it may constitute one of the items in grading.

Following a story discussion, the students may feel the need to invite a resource person in order to explore some particular aspect of the story's theme requiring highly specialized knowledge or experience.

Field trips may be an appropriate follow-up to a story discussion. Some opportunities for first-hand observation may be close at hand, as, for example, the neighborhood playground, the supermarket, the marriage-license bureau. A visit to a divorce court, a counseling center, or a children's ward may precede as well as follow a class meeting. Panel reports by a group of students may permit the whole class to share in an experience that cannot be offered to a large group.

Evaluation

The teacher will wish to check his impressions of how useful the class has found each story. This can be done by offering the students an anonymous evaluation form either periodically or at the end of the term. Each student can respond frankly, indicating which stories he found of most and which of least benefit. Since this involves the problem of recall, the teacher may seek more immediate reactions by inquiring, toward the end of a class meeting, "Do you think this is a story we should continue to assign?"

The teacher's evaluation of student growth, either for grading or for guidance purposes, must be based, in the new course, as in family courses generally, on both teacher estimate and student self-report. To acquire bases for estimate other than classroom performance, the teacher can give mid-term and end-term examinations that test the student's ability to relate the instance of the story to broader psychological and sociological principles. It is also possible to test empathic skill by asking the students to analyze a story they had not read before the examination. Questions can also be formulated to test student ability to relate one story to another. While examination questions will usually reflect the teacher's emphasis on particular psychological or sociological approaches, the following are offered as a few general examples:

1. What similarities and contrasts between Anastasia and her old aunt are shown in "Family Scene" so far as the opportunities and the problems of the unmarried woman are concerned?

2. Discuss several approaches to the problem of premarital sexual intercourse, including the difficulties and the advantages that characterize each of them. Illustrate from "Winter Term," "None Sing So Wildly," and "A Country Weekend."

3. In what ways do "Love and Like" and "We're All Guests" illuminate the following problems: (a) mate selection in remarriage; and (b) visiting privileges for parents who are separated or divorced?

4. What are the father's feelings about the infant in "My Oedipus Complex" and how do they reflect the historical epoch, the socio-economic group, and the culture setting? Compare and contrast with

current middle-class conceptions of the father role in the United States.

5. Frank feels conflicting emotions at several points in "The Apple Tree." What are these emotions and how does he settle the conflict in each instance?

6. "Uncle Wiggily in Connecticut" illuminates a number of concepts and issues in family study: maternal role, in-law relationships, suburban family life, marital communication, halo effect, fantasy playmate, the emotionally broken home. Choose one and discuss it, relating the specific instance of the story to your textbook reading, class discussion, and other work in the course.

SUMMARY

Stories can be used either in ongoing courses or in a new course based primarily on fiction. In the former, stories can play a minor or a major role, illuminating few or many family themes and serving as a discussion focus or as the basis for written report and examination. In the new course, story discussion is central and accordingly requires teacher and student role modifications in the direction of participation and cooperation. The design of the new course in family study can utilize any variant of the individual or the family life cycle. While it will generally incude most of the content areas for which stories are offered in Part II, it may select among a wide array of subthemes.

In the new course and in ongoing courses, it is desirable to devote one class meeting to orientation and demonstration in order to clarify procedures and expectations. Preparatory and follow-up experiences in the examination of stories will differ in the two situations mainly in matter of degree: to the extent that classroom discussion is not feasible in the ongoing course there is more reliance on written work or panel reports whereas the new course, based on student interaction in the classroom, may make more use of buzz groups and role-playing, asking for written work mainly in the academic setting which requires grades or any setting which uses stories for individual guidance purposes. The new course designed for non-credit students may eliminate written work entirely, although it will be found that students ordinarily threatened by such requirements accept the responsibility with less anxiety when story characters are their focus. This is of particular value when courses are intended to serve as a bridge between non-academic activity and formal study.

PART II

STORIES FOR THE MAJOR
CONTENT AREAS OF FAMILY STUDY

Introduction

Those aspects of family relationship that are considered basic in American society are included in most textbooks in the field, differ as they may in the kind and length of treatment. Chapters or parts of chapters are devoted to ten major areas: the changing roles of men and women, adolescents and young adults, dating and mate selection, sex standards, the unmarried adult, marital adjustment, parent-child and sibling relationships, family disorganization, aging and the aged, and bereavement.

Since the textbooks are intended to meet course needs, and since surveys have found that most courses make use of textbooks along with reference materials, it can be assumed that most courses include much the same content areas. Examination of the syllabi of family courses offered in colleges in widely scattered parts of the country provides some confirmation for this assumption.

The stories chosen for summarization and for listing have been arranged under headings that allow synchronization with textbook chapters and thereby facilitate their use in ongoing courses. Because the sequence also has a certain logic in terms of the marital life cycle, it can also constitute one of the alternative designs of a new family course. Such a course, offering stories as the major reading assignments, with sociological and psychological readings as supplementary, is offered at the New School for Social Research on a two-semester basis under the title, "Family Interaction: Insights through the Short Story."

In each of the ten content sections there will be three kinds of story listings. Under "Selections" are listed the two or three stories for which summaries are to follow a brief section introduction. Under "See Also" those stories are listed which are summarized in other content areas but are pertinent in this as well. Under "Reserve" are listed the stories which are mentioned in the section introduction but are not given detailed summaries. "Reserve" stories, too, may be listed in several content sections, since a story may focus on more than one family theme, offering illuminating sidelights on several. (In all listings, only titles are given. Full bibliographical data will be found in Appendix A.)

For each summarized story a listing of "discussion themes" is intended to suggest the varied potential available. The teacher may wish to secure the total contribution which a story can make by recalling it in other contexts from the one for which it was originally assigned. In this way the student's reading can be of multiple service. A story examined earlier in the semester can add a new dimension to one currently under discussion. This is particularly helpful when controversial issues or complex phenomena are involved, for class time rarely permits the assignment of the many stories needed to suggest the variables that affect the consequences. If "The Bronco-Buster" has already been assigned for its tragic illumination of the problem of independence-training, it still has much to offer about the working mother in a lower socioeconomic setting, usefully supplementing what "A Country Weekend" reveals about career women in upper middle-class society.

The story summaries in each content section are intended to aid the teacher in at least two ways. First, they may help him make a selection among the stories that corresponds closely to the interests and needs of his particular classes. Secondly, references to the key personal relationships and the significant social forces revealed in the story may suggest various questions which the teacher can formulate to move the class discussion toward clarification of feelings and motivations of story characters or toward consideration of the social framework of the family, or both, depending on the degree of psychological or sociological emphasis in the course. If the summary has interested the teacher enough to make him read the story, and the reading has confirmed his choice, he may bring to class only an enumeration of the key problems raised by the story. It is widely agreed that the best questions are those spontaneously asked under the immediate impetus of discussion.

All the stories listed in the following sections, whether summarized or not, have been used in family and related courses (psychology of adolescence, introductory sociology, family interaction, and family relationships) in the variety of ways discussed in Part I, and can be recommended for the insights and enjoyment they contribute to the study of human relationships.

1

The Changing Roles
of Men and Women

Few stories focus directly on the changing roles of men and women in industrialized society, although new concepts of masculinity and femininity are basic to consideration of modern courtship, child-rearing, and marital adjustment. "Peace for Geretiello" and "Twenty-one," translated from the Italian and the Norwegian respectively, both deal with patriarchal family patterns, but in two variants. In the one, women do not participate in social production; in the other, more characteristic of rural societies, women may work outside the home, occasionally in gainful employment but more usually in tasks associated with the family farm. Both stories, however, with their sharp role allocations provide a baseline for discussion of the changes that have accompanied large-scale industry and brought about a more equalitarian family pattern.

Role changes may be due not only to environmental factors but to the personality of an individual. "The Apple Tree," although primarily focused on romantic love and the socioeconomic barrier in

31

mate selection, offers an instance of conventional outward sex attributes combined with subtly but unmistakably reversed roles in
decision making.

"Wife of the Hero" provokes discussion of how changing roles
affect dating choices and parent-adolescent relationships. Although
the story is somewhat dated, it poses a question that is still pertinent:
is it enough to become the wife of a hero, a man who contributes to
social progress, or has the young woman an obligation to find fulfillment on her own merits? The students are challenged by the story
to examine their own role expectations and to measure them against
the recent assertion of Simone de Beauvoir: "Everything still encourages the young girl to expect fortune and happiness from some
Prince Charming rather than to attempt by herself their difficult and
uncertain conquest."

"A Country Weekend" offers a bleak view of what happens when
a woman does make this attempt. The view is indirect for the story
is, perhaps, more concerned with paternal overattachment and premarital sexual relations. Nonetheless, consideration of the career
wife (a social anthropologist in the story), not driven by economic
necessity, can lead to a discussion of several propositions that have
relevance for the college student in relation to study and mate selection goals: (1) women may have a contribution to make to society
by working outside the home; (2) for many women it is a desirable
role because of differences in women's psychological needs, some
finding contentment in homemaking, others becoming unsatisfied
and unsatisfactory wives and mothers when forced wholly into domestic roles; and (3) societies differ in the degree of guilt they in-
still in women who choose one role rather than the other as well as
in the degree of cooperation offered the working woman. Although
editorializing weakens the creative power of the story, the very fact
that the author is so eager to condemn the wife allows the students
to see their own eagerness to conclude, despite conflicting clues, as
does the author, that all the family maladjustments derive from the
mother's career absences. If the students have, in their concentration
on a working-mother scapegoat, ignored the contrasting character
in the story, the discontented woman of education who stays at home,
the teacher's questions may help move the discussion in this direction.

"Family Scene," concerned with the unmarried adult and her relations with mother and with siblings, is useful in showing how the
new roles open to women also permit their exploitation by other
family members even in a society that retains much of its traditional

sex role orientation. This story, also translated from the Italian, contrasts illuminatingly with "Peace for Geretiello," revealing the significance of family subcultures in role interpretation.

While "Moses Supposes" is most useful in the study of marital adjustment and family disorganization, it is also helpful in examining the role allocations in college marriages when economic dependency and unexpected pregnancy are factors in the situation.

"Bitter Honeymoon" reveals the challenge that new roles bring in the form of new associations. A wife's relationships with male colleagues at work or in politics may intensify feelings of jealousy. It is evident also that earlier assumptions of identity of values are no longer tenable when husband and wife have the right to develop their individual convictions.

"A Day's Wooing" shows that the rigid role allocations of an earlier day sometimes placed the initiative in fumbling hands. The setting of the story is rural lower-lower class but it stimulates an examination of changing roles in dating and courtship at all social levels.

"The Gay Old Dog," because it is somewhat dated, points up the change in the man's responsibility for economic support of sisters.

"Mother to Dinner," focused primarily on marriage adjustment and parent-adolescent relationships, permits discussion of the contribution a work role can make in lessening the young wife's emotional dependence on family members.

Possibly the earliest of the "office wife" stories, "Two Bluebirds" reveals the precarious position of the upper middle-class wife whose role may be largely ornamental compared with the work role of her husband's assistant.

The marked increase in the number and proportion of women gainfully employed since the beginning of the war years makes it likely that most students will have some first-hand experience with the situation in which a woman family member shares the provider role and the man shares the expressive function. Student feelings as a result of that experience are often confused, if not wholly negative. Through story discussion, some perspective is gained both on the magnitude of the domestic revolution and the individual's relation to it. Once they see confusion about sex roles, not as personal inadequacy, but as growing pains that accompany greater maturity, the students are relieved of some of their anxiety and can begin to appreciate the opportunity, in contrast with previous patriarchal limitations, for broadened interpersonal horizons within the family

unit. In this new context the students may also recognize the legiti-
macy of some of their original discomfort and accept the fact that
the new flexibility makes more complex demands on each individual.
With new insights derived from story discussion, the student often
responds well to a written assignment that asks him to contrast the
roles open to him with those open to a grandparent of the same sex.
This helps bring the play of large social forces into personal focus
for him.

"PEACE FOR GERETIELLO"

Discussion Themes:

Family patterns: patriarchal
Family size
The dowry: old forms and new
Role allocations by sex
Sons and daughters
Sexual deviancy
Old age and retirement

Geretiello, seventy-six years of age, and still serving as beach at-
tendant on his native isle of Capri, is increasingly embittered by the
menial tasks he continues to undertake in order to earn large tips.
On the surface friendly and respectful, he shows his feelings only at
home. All through the years he has encouraged his wife and seven
daughters to share his hostility toward those he serves. Daily, over
the family meal, he recounts the activities of the wealthy sex deviants
and the boastfully promiscuous men and women who frequent the
resort.

His stress on their shortcomings may serve several purposes. It
enhances his own family's virtue; it cloaks his envy of a leisured
existence; but perhaps above all, it makes him the focus of family
attention, for his sordid tales are the one connection the sheltered
women of his family have with the outside world.

His need for money through the years has been intensified by his
determination to provide ample dowries for all the daughters. His
retirement is now delayed as he toils to amass an especially imposing
dowry for the last daughter still in the parental home. What seems
to be a self-punishing interpretation of community expectations may
represent his need for self-aggrandizement, a desire to play a munifi-
cent and patronizing role to offset the humiliating character of his

daily work. It has brought him hardships, but also ego satisfactions he may not otherwise have attained in a life of severely limited economic and educational opportunity.

Geretiello's wife and daughters react to his frustrating control over them and their role limitation by making constant demands on him for clothes, venting their unacknowledged anger in a socially acceptable way, as if to say, if he is so strong, let him bear more burdens.

When Geretiello dies one warm day at the beach, he is described by those he detested as kindly and friendly. This perception of him may help them maintain their self-images as likable people rather than mere purchasers of services. If he can be seen as having been happy in serving them, it may also help relieve guilt feelings over their use of the aged man.

"TWENTY-ONE"

Discussion Themes:

Community mores
Cross-cultural comparisons
Family patterns: patriarchal
Father-son relationships
Mothers-in-law
Premarital sex: Scandinavian pattern
Mate selection: parental roles
Family life: rural
Sibling rivalry
Romantic love
Role discontinuities: age milestones

The young man, never named in the story, is on the eve of his twenty-first birthday. His brother Olaf is a year older. Together with the girl Hild, they are working in the barley fields. Hild's family is new in the district but because of their industrious reputation they have without difficulty found work on neighboring farms. Hild has been brought to this farm not for her labor alone, but as a possible wife for one of the brothers. They are both attracted to her. The younger man feels unable to compete with his brother in small attentions to the girl. But with his twenty-first birthday, a significant milestone in the culture, he is supported by a new feeling of adulthood and takes the decisive step of inviting Hild to meet him alone in the evening.

2

Adolescents and Young Adults

Adolescence is a favorite subject of short-story writers. In many instances they are recalling their own difficulties of growing up and coping with role discontinuities that are characteristic of American society. As a content area in family study it contains considerable overlap with others, for the developmental tasks of adolescence are generally taken to include some growth in independence from the family, movement from one-sex groups to heterosexual relationships, establishment of self-identity, and choice of educational and occupational goals. Characters in their teens and early twenties are therefore frequently key figures in stories about mate selection, parent-child and sibling relationships, sexual standards, family disorganization, aging and bereavement. The joys of adolescence are little explored in any of the stories, but the college student seems not to object to the fictional emphasis on confusion and suffering in his age period. It may be reassuring to him in terms of normality, for he is rarely at ease in his current relationships with friends, family, dating partners, teachers, and the draft board.

In "The Bronco-Buster" a boy in early adolescence from a home marked by economic hardship and desertion finds it difficult to cope with adult demands, and perishes. In "The Wife of a Hero" a girl in later adolescence in a more favored economic situation is not jeopardized in physical survival but in the ability to live by values that may challenge her family's preferences.

The problem of independence-training can be further explored in "Truth and Consequences," in which a boy begins to realize that he is fulfilling his mother's, not his own, professional aspirations.

The sexual awakening of the adolescent is the theme of "Eighteenth Summer" and "That Lovely Green Boat." "A Week of Roses" depicts the disillusionment of an adolescent who has a "crush" on his mother's friend of college days.

Many stories reveal the intensification of the problems of the adolescent under conditions of family crisis. Foster care in the absence of parents is the background situation in "A Mountain Summer," involving two young brothers, and in "In the Zoo" which concerns two sisters. "We're All Guests" and "A Red-Letter Day" show young adolescents of upper middle-class background reacting to the divorce of their parents. In "Who Lives Alas Away" the loss of a beloved older brother becomes overwhelming to a young adolescent girl when her parents are too preoccupied with their own grief to provide emotional support.

"Twenty-one" offers an instance when age milestones in a culture aid in the development of the adolescent's self-concept.

The adolescent's need for an adult friend in times of stress is not easily satisfied in the midst of academic pressures that operate on the adults themselves, "The Colleagues of Mr. Chips" makes tragically evident.

"THE BRONCO-BUSTER"

Discussion Themes:

Mother-son relationships
Independence training
Desertion
Remarriage
Peer groups
One-parent family
Working mother
Family and school
Alcoholism

When Frankie talks about getting a motorcycle, his mother threatens to send him to live with his alcoholic father who deserted them when the boy was four or five years old. Frankie at first contents himself with daydreaming about motorcycle adventures but when his mother begins to ignore him in favor of a widower, he starts to save the money he earns working in a delicatessen after school.

Frankie's mother has been an overpowering figure in his life. Angry at her husband's desertion and wearied by long hours at a menial job and sole responsibility for the boy, she makes Frankie feel guilty about being male and about making decisions of his own. He does poorly in school, makes few friends, is disinterested in girls.

He is not prepared for his mother's sudden lack of interest in him when she contemplates remarriage. He sees this as a kind of second parental desertion, with further impairment to his self-image. At sixteen, he is faced with two decisions: whether to buy a motorcycle suddenly available and risk his mother's disapproval; and, having bought it, whether to refuse to mount it and reveal his ignorance of its workings. The latter course would risk the disapproval of the truck drivers urging him on, and Frankie has never learned to cope with the demands adults make on him. His usual compliant response precipitates the tragedy previously seen in fantasy when loneliness made him hunger for the attention death would bring. The death wish implied in his suicidal assent to ride the powerful vehicle may have had roots in his sense of guilt which made him seek punishment for making a decision counter to his mother's.

"WIFE OF THE HERO"

Discussion Themes:

Changing roles of men and women
Dating: socioeconomic factors
Family values
Young adults
Mate selection: family influences
Parent-adolescent relationships

Libby, living in a wealthy suburban community, comes to the city when she has dates with Joe. She enjoys being with him because, unlike the boys in her own crowd, he talks to her about serious matters. When her parents insist on her bringing him home so they may meet him, she gives him up. Otherwise she will have to reveal to her

Hollywood-minded sister of seventeen and to her parents with their conventional country-club interests that her description of him has been false, cast in the image of what would be acceptable to them. That he is short, without a car, with a farm background, graduate of an obscure college would lower their estimate of her as well as of him. She can also anticipate Joe's criticism of her family. This might precipitate her into an examination she is not yet able to undertake, because she is still too dependent on her parents to recognize openly any of their shortcomings or to challenge any of their assumptions. Her decision to part with Joe leaves her guilty and confused.

3

Dating and
Mate Selection

Selections:
  The Apple Tree
  A Country Weekend

See also:
  Faces of Hatred and of Love
  Late in the Season
  Moses Supposes
  None Sing So Wildly
  Twenty-one
  We're All Guests
  Wife of the Hero

Reserve:
  The Best of Everything
  Bitter Honeymoon
  The Colleagues of Mr. Chips
  A Day's Wooing
  It's an Old Story
  Jack the Greatest
  The Magic Barrel
  The Peacocks of Avignon

The significance of the choice of a marriage partner has intensified with increasing longevity, early completion of child bearing and child rearing, and the greater affectional expectations in the family of highly industrialized societies. Although the elements of social homogamy—so frankly recognized in the arranged marriage of more traditional societies—can be found to persist even where individual freedom of choice is proclaimed, a new emphasis on personal compatibility and on self-fulfillment for both mates makes the selection of a husband or a wife a great responsibility.

The many stories available in this area aid the exploration of the complexities of the mate choice process. Additional insights can be gained in stories of marital adjustment, of parent-child relationships, of separation and divorce. The passing years reveal motivations and characteristics not always evident in the courtship period. Stories

40

serve thereby to provide greater depth and perspective in family study, offsetting a tendency, noted by family life educators, for college students to be impatient of course time devoted to the later years. Stories from the other content areas permit mate selection to be seen as only one factor in a satisfying marriage; some appreciation is gained of the need to grow throughout the years rather than depend on initial compatibility.

With early dating and early marriage as major trends in American courtship, stories recommended in the preceding section (on Adolescents) can be helpful in exploring the problem of marriage-readiness. That chronological age has different meaning in various cultural contexts is evident in the contrast between "Twenty-one" and "The Colleagues of Mr. Chips." The latter also warns against underestimating the impact of dating failure on adolescent feelings of worth and acceptability.

"The Apple Tree" treats, in a lyrical setting, the conflicting needs of a young man to satisfy the values of his reference groups and to fulfill his own poetic bent. The story makes it evident that mate-selection requires of the individual a life philosophy, a set of convictions, a reckoning with value priorities, a confrontation of personal inadequacy. Any tendency of the students to avoid the issue by references to the more rigid stratification in English society can be turned to good account by inquiring into the social and personal pressures that would come into operation if an American youth were in a similar situation. It will become clear that Pygmalion is as rare as Horatio Alger in contemporary life.

"None Sing So Wildly" also illuminates the difficulty of reconciling conflicting needs for security and adventure in choosing a mate. The broken engagement suggests the value of sufficient courtship time in which to test out the mutuality of expectations and goals.

Divergences of values emerge in "Bitter Honeymoon" too, with the added dimension of the threat to the male ego in woman's new role, her involvement with colleagues and causes outside his interests.

"A Country Weekend," by presenting an extreme degree of reluctance on the part of a father to see his daughter transfer her affections to another male, permits examination of the normal ambivalence that may characterize parents in the mate-selection period.

In "Twenty-one" there is reliance upon parental judgment combined with male initiative in a patriarchal setting. "A Day's Wooing" also shows the rigid role allocations in traditional courting behaviors.

"Moses Supposes" and "Jack the Greatest" point up how for some college students as well as other youths the comfort and reassurance once sought in the family of orientation is expected to be realized in the setting up of a new family unit. Initial marital adjustments are shown to relate to the mate selected as well as to the individual's own personality and situation, in the one instance in a college setting and in the other on the eve of compulsory military service.

"Late in the Season" suggests the diversity of motivations for entering marriage, with the desire for children sometimes overriding other considerations in the choice of a mate.

"Faces of Hatred and of Love" exposes the furtive nature of courtship, the barrier to free communication between the pair, when marriage is being used as an escape from parental domination. "It's an Old Story" also deals with a mother's overinvolvement in her son but stresses the immobilization induced in him when the valences of mother and mate relationships are equally compelling. These two stories, together with "Jack the Greatest," illuminate the problem of mate selection in the one-parent family.

"Wife of the Hero" presents the indirect influences on mate selection exercised by the family of origin. "A Day's Wooing" reveals the barrier the family represents to a diffident suitor.

"The Best of Everything" suggests that the individual's sense of worth is as important a factor in marital aspiration as in other life choices. The lower-middle-class characters in this story point up effectively several contrasts with the mate choice considerations of more affluent and educated characters in several other stories.

"The Magic Barrel" has a young rabbinical student examine the photographs and biographies of a number of eligible young women sponsored by a marriage broker, still a prominent figure in matchmaking. The sad-comic process of weeding out the candidates prompts class discussion of many material and spiritual aspects of choice. It also permits exploration of such themes as accepted modes of introduction in various cultures and subcultures, the kinds of parental involvement in the mate-selection process, and self-understanding as the first requisite of mate-selection.

Choosing a mate in remarriage is an increasingly common phenomenon. "We're All Guests" points up one significant aspect, when children of the first marriage also have to be wooed. "The Peacocks of Avignon" also shows the impact on offspring but in this instance it is compassion for the widowed mother that allows an older daughter to accept the challenging choice made.

"THE APPLE TREE"

Discussion Themes:

Premarital sexual relations
Romantic love
The silver wedding anniversary
Social homogamy
Dominance-submission: spousal roles
Parent images
Family life: rural

Frank and Stella Ashurst are driving toward a resort town on the English coast where they had first met more than twenty-five years ago. Stella chooses the place to stop for a picnic lunch. Frank is passive and uncommunicative, as usual.

The lovely spot arouses a vague sense of discontent in Frank, a sense of waste, and he begins to recall the events of long ago, when at the age of twenty-two he had been on a walking trip to mark the end of college studies. Staying at a nearby farm, he had been attracted to Megan. Her beauty and her love of nature made her unlike the farm family to whom she was related and for whom she had worked since coming from her native Wales. Chivalric feelings had prevented Frank's taking advantage of Megan's simple and uncalculating willingness. He assures her they will get married in London, and goes to the nearby resort town of Torquay to get cash at the bank and to purchase a travel outfit for her.

His basic ambivalence about the marriage is intensified when he meets a friend, Phil Halliday, and his sisters, including Stella. Frank delays his return to the farm and when Megan comes to Torquay to search for him, he hides, rationalizing away as conceit on his part the knowledge that Megan will take hard his unexplained desertion of her. He also expresses through a quarrel with the Hallidays the anger he feels at his own conduct, but he soon resumes his friendship with them.

It is only now, a quarter of a century later, that he learns of Megan's suicide. The sadness he feels is mainly for the "beauty and rapture" he had failed to experience. He is able to protect himself from recognition of guilt in Megan's death by forgetting the broken promise to marry her and assuring himself it was his virtue that had caused the tragedy. He evades confrontation of his pattern of passivity—not daring has brought about his not caring to control his own fate. Stella accepts the dominant role in family decision making.

"A COUNTRY WEEKEND"

Discussion Themes:

Dating and courtship
Parents and suitors
Marital adjustment: middle years
Premarital sexual relations
Infidelity and adultery
The only child
Working wives and mothers
Family friendships

Constance Browning, a graduate student planning to teach in nursery school, is spending the weekend with her father who is a psychiatrist, her friend Spencer, and the Stissings who have a country house nearby. Connie's mother is away on a field trip as a cultural anthropologist; she is studying marriage among the Andean Indians. Connie is apprehensive about announcing her engagement to Spencer, because she realizes that her father has an unrecognized need to keep her from an affectionate relationship with any other man. She reveals to Spencer that she was once engaged, that this relationship had been precipitated by her father's discovery of her weekends alone with the young man, and that the engagement had been broken after her father had succeeded in making her fiance feel inferior.

Dr. Browning's affair with Mrs. Stissing has helped weaken his authority over Connie. She chooses to announce her engagement to Spencer when her father may be too immobilized by his own sense of guilt to interfere with her plans. Connie and Spencer have managed to build up a strong bond of respect and affection, indicating very different motivations and consequences for their sexual relationship than had characterized her earlier experience.

4

Sex
Standards

Each society develops its characteristic ways of handling the sexual needs of young people before marriage. Some enjoin total abstinence; some, abstinence for one sex; some proscribe promiscuity but accept sexual relations based on affection; others set only broad limits of time, place, degree of kinship. Murdock's study of a worldwide sample of 250 societies reveals sexual experimentation before marriage to be commonly accepted. Christiansen shows the toleration of premarital sexual relations in Scandinavian countries to be part of a courtship tradition, occurring not only later in the lives of college youth than in the lives of their American counterparts, but in a different social context of attitude and commitment. In most cross-cultural studies there were found to be few marked differences between individual practices and social norms.

45

In contrast, Kinsey and his colleagues brought into public consciousness the degree to which sexual rules in the United States—supported more or less consistently by a variety of social institutions: the law, the church, the school, and the family—were being ignored in actual practice, if not in feelings of guilt and mistrust. Norm confusions have multiplied as American society has grown more sharply stratified, with standards as well as practices becoming differentiated among the various socioeconomic and educational groups. Religious and ethnic subcultures have further complicated the problems of consistency of social expectation. Family life educators debate whether consensus can be reached on enforceable norms for adolescents and whether enforcement is feasible for the older adolescent now freed from chaperonage by the auto, the anonymity of urbanization, and the dominance of peer group culture. Some, like Kirkendall, maintain that only inner controls, deriving from a sense of responsibility for the welfare of others, can provide effective safeguards against the promiscuity that many family life educators consider a threat to the individual's capacity to establish close relationships.

Some, like Albert Ellis and Murdock, doubt the desirability of premarital abstinence, the former in terms of the individual and the latter in terms of society. Murdock declares: "Most peoples have clearly found sexual permissiveness before marriage quite compatible with postmarital fidelity and with the stability and adequate functioning of the family institution." Woodward points out that anthropological findings may have little significance for policy determination in other societies, that transplantation requires similar soil: "May it not be true that an ideal of premarital chastity has more significance in a society that insists that sexual intercourse be an experience of mutual and lasting affection . . . ?" Moreover, while many sociologists and psychologists maintain that the mass media in a society exacerbate the problem by using human sexual instincts to sell products, few have dared to suggest how that society may bell a cat that may be its own mirror image.

The student approaches this area of family study seeking clarification of his own impulses and the social norms, hoping to develop a defensible set of values concerning sexual relationships. The short story is effective in revealing the many motivations and outcomes of sexual activity and enables the student to examine critically the various generalizations about premarital sexuality. "Winter Term" shows the loneliness that may drive a college girl into acts for which she has little biological need and which she does not find pleasurable.

It also shows the threat to the accomplishment of other adolescent tasks, notably intellectual growth and peer group relations. "None Sing So Wildly" stresses the negative consequences when the girl uses her sexual attractions in a barter to gain a man's conformity to her more conventional occupational goals. "The Apple Tree" touches on cross-class sexual involvement. "Twenty-one" suggests the Scandinavian pattern of sexual relations as part of courtship commitment. Perhaps "A Country Weekend" comes closest to illustrating the view that joint growth can ensue when a sexual relationship before marriage is based on strong affection, respect, and readiness to take responsibility for the consequences.

Sexual deviancy can be explored through "Peace for Geretiello" and "Saul." Although, according to Kinsey, homosexuality is of low incidence in college years, the subject is not without importance in relation to earlier and later periods. "Saul" permits a brief glimpse of latent and overt homosexuality, shedding some light on family relationships as a causal factor and the mechanism of denial as a significant component of social attitudes toward deviancy.

"News for the Church" questions the use of fear and shame in controlling sexual behavior. "That Lovely Green Boat" suggests the vulnerability of the very young adolescent, allowing some discussion of the supervision needed by different age groups. In "Eighteenth Summer" the differing standards of two social groups bring to the fore the relationship between promiscuity and popularity, and the general expectation that the female has primary responsibility in setting sexual standards in dating. "The Best of Everything" handles ironically the heightened feelings on the wedding eve.

The issue of prostitution can be explored through "The Paper House." Its foreign setting permits discussion of the status of the prostitute in different societies, the different motivation in affluent and poor economies, and the relationships among various kinds of sexual exploitation.

Problems of sexual standards after marriage are suggested in many of the stories listed in the areas of marital adjustment and family disorganization. Cross-cultural expectations can be explored in "The Fall of Candida" and adultery in "The Prophecy." "The Human Element" shows sex separated from love as an upper class woman exploits her chauffeur to avoid assuming the obligations of a multidimensional relationship.

The difficulty parents find in providing adequate sex education for their children is evident in "My Oedipus Complex" and in "The Picnic."

The issue of modesty in husband-wife relationships is raised in "Revelation." Although somewhat dated, this story in a Welsh setting provokes discussion of changing standards through the centuries and in different societies. Modesty as a disguise for other feelings is suggested in "A Week of Roses."

"WINTER TERM"

Discussion Themes:

College dating
College holidays
College regulations
Guidance services
Premarital sexual relations
Adolescents

Ellie and Hal have been meeting in the library each evening in the winter term of the college year. Little studying is done. Hal is concerned about the deterioriation of his grades and the loss of his earlier feeling of intellectual accomplishment. With an examination coming up he wants to leave Ellie at her dormitory early and get to studying. Ellie, lonely and unable to find companionship among the girls, is desperate at the prospect of losing Hal so early in the evening, and contrives so to rouse him as they kiss good-night that his resolution to study is partly forgotten. Only partly, however, as the hostility he feels in this surrender finds expression in the violence of his approach to her in the sordid setting of a parking lot.

"NONE SING SO WILDLY"

Discussion Themes:

The artist in the family
Engagement
In-laws
Marriage and friendships
Middle-class values
Premarital sexual relations

Van Merrick and Norma Fry are planning to be married in the spring when Van's novel is finished. His choosing to write rather than take a conventional job makes his future in-laws dubious of him.

Norma, too, would prefer his taking some work that would allow them to marry without delay, particularly as she is worried lest her parents discover she and Van have been having sexual relations.

Van and Norma quarrel frequently. Both are uneasy. Norma is vaguely aware that she is hoping marriage will bring Van around to the values her family hold primary. She senses that she has been using sex as an instrument in her relationship with Van. He at twenty-six enjoys the feeling of security she brings into his adventurous life but is somewhat fearful of marriage as a possible threat to his goals. From encounters with people like Norma's father in houses of prostitution he has become familiar with the hypocrisy of many conventional marriages. Van's way of life, his choosing not to go to officers' school, his friendships with beatniks, his indifference to physical comfort, his absorption in his writing, would all suggest the need for a wife who is similarly indifferent to many middle-class values. He is suspicious that behind Norma's seeming willingness to join him in such a life pattern lies a hidden intention of reforming him.

The divergence of values is finally brought into the open by an incident at the shore in which another young couple is subjected to indignities. Van wants to help them and Norma insists that he stay out of the matter. His need to defy authority, to be active in structuring the world along lines of principle, contrasts with Norma's difficulty in defying power figures and in finding values worth defending. In the quarrel that follows and ends their engagement, Norma and Van both feel the angrier because they had half-suspected they could not reconcile in their choice of each other the conflicting needs each has for security and for adventure.

5

The
Unmarried Adult

"Failure to marry" is a phrase that conveys society's disapproval of men and women who do not conform to the expectation that they will join in matrimony and found new family units. Fiction helps to mitigate the common judgmental approach. The stories show the diversity of causal factors in the decision not to marry.

The avoidance of marriage is often tied to prior relationships with family members. Sometimes the parental marriage has disillusioned the children as to the satisfactions to be found in home life. More frequently, the mother has overattached herself to a child, either to find emotional compensation or financial support, and operates consciously or unconsciously to hamper the process of mate selection. This is particularly common where the mother has lost her spouse, through death or divorce, or does not have a satisfying relationship in an intact family. Sometimes the deviance from the norm of attractiveness for the given society or community renders the individual more vulnerable to the machinations of those who can exploit

his singlehood. "Family Scene" combines several of these possibilities, with the eldest daughter the more easily used as the family's
financial support because she is aware of her lack of beauty. This
story, laid in Italy, contrasts the alternatives open to unmarried
women of an earlier day and today. "Bridgeport Bus" has elements
of similarity in the way the mother-daughter relationship underlies
inability to marry but presents a daughter with a higher level of
awareness and more overt hostility to a rejecting and exploitative
mother.

"Main Currents in American Thought" shows subtle manipulation
by a mother to make her son take on the responsibilities not ade-
quately shouldered by the father. It also suggests that the role the
son is placed in is so satisfying to him that he does not try to achieve
independence. This ambivalence is also underlined in "It's an Old
Story" and in "The Gay Old Dog." In the latter the loneliness of
later years is stressed and the tendency of the unmarried individual
to blame those for whom he made his sacrifices, forgetting the satisfaction he had derived from accepting the role.

"Eveline" suggests the attachment to a father that will keep a
daughter from ever accepting offers of marriage. "A New England
Nun" shows the individual getting set in her ways and experiencing
relief when she can escape entering a relationship that will require
habit changes and constant adjustment to the needs and preferences
of another person.

"The Blind Man" suggests the neurotic component in an unmarried man's make-up that does not permit him to form a close attachment to any individual, even the intimacy of a friendship constituting
a threat.

What "The Bridgeport Bus" reveals about a mother-daughter relationship, "Everything That Rises Must Converge" illuminates in
the mother-son relationship, with the need to take revenge for griev-
ances, real and imagined, transcending most other needs, including
that of marriage. The mother-son family is treated humorously in
"Childybawn" and the marriage of the son at 46 permits discussion
of the contrasting conceptions of spinsterhood and bachelorhood in
Irish culture and in others.

"None Sing So Wildly" calls attention to special life styles that
make conventional marriage difficult to maintain. "Late in the Season" suggests the near panic that seizes the woman as her child-
bearing years diminish. "Faces of Hatred and of Love" shows the
gratitude of the unmarried woman who at last is courted. "A Week

of Roses" develops subtly the likelihood that inability to accept a sexual role underlies some singleness

There seem to be few stories that stress any of the positive elements either in the choice to remain single, as in religious or political commitment, or in the opportunities for the unmarried to fulfill their needs for sex, tenderness, relation to children, and everyday companionship within present institutional arrangements and public and private attitudes.

"FAMILY SCENE"

Discussion Themes:

Changing roles of men and women
Illness in the family
Aging: role reversal
Ordinal position in the family
The rejecting mother
The unmarried woman
Self-concepts: family and community influences
One-parent family

Anastasia Finizio, at thirty-eight, supports the whole family: mother, aunt, sister Anna, eighteen, and two brothers Eduardo, thirty, and Petrillo, sixteen. The level of health is poor for Anastasia's siblings and there is every prospect that the approaching weddings of Anna and of Eduardo will bring new family responsibilities for Anastasia.

When Anastasia hears that Antonio Laurano, thirty-two, is back in Naples and sends his regards to her, she has sudden hopes of ending her spinsterhood. Tall, thin, large-boned, in a society that does not consider these as attributes of beauty, Anastasia suffers also from the insecurity that derives from maternal rejection. It is not difficult for the mother to bring Anastasia's self-doubts into play and to ensure thereby continued financial support for the family. The old aunt, assigned to a servile role in the family, represents the more limited possibilities open to the unmarried woman in the previous generation. Anastasia has, by way of contrast, her "successful career, expensive clothes, and the satisfaction of being the mainstay of so many people."

"BRIDGEPORT BUS"

Discussion Themes:

Self-concepts: family and community influences
Sibling rivalry
Mother-daughter relationships
The unmarried woman
Widowhood
One-parent family

Mary Agnes, exceptionally tall and gaunt, lives with her widowed mother in a house purchased with the money her father had set aside for her college education. Ag has not only the problem of physical unattractiveness but strong resentment of her mother's open preference for her brother. The intellectual defense against her own feelings serves Ag in a dual capacity. All the evening college courses Ag takes are resented by the mother who would prefer a daughter interested in sharing her own world of gossip and religious ritual. Ag threatens to get on a Bridgeport bus and ride away from the obligation of supporting her mother, but this is only a consoling fantasy to disguise her entwinement in a love-hate relationship that must keep her close to the rejecting mother. Ag begins to write, and it is possible that this will be a therapeutic experience for her.

"MAIN CURRENTS IN AMERICAN THOUGHT"

Discussion Themes:

The artist in the family
Courtship
Middle-class values
Siblings
Mother-son relationships
The unmarried man

Andrew, at twenty-five is writing pulp fiction while notes he once made for a play gather dust on his desk. His mother, sister, and father make constant financial demands on him. Andrew resents the responsibility and, fearing to add to his burdens, decides not to marry Martha, a girl from a poor family.

Andrew feels trapped but the satisfactions he gains from being the pivot of the family's existence, of living a comfortable, middle-class life, of maintaining a special status as a writer, are sufficient to keep him from actively seeking the satisfactions of independence and literary creativity.

His mother thinks of herself as allowing Andrew a free choice but unconsciously binds him so closely to her that he is unable to take a decisive step to end his frustration.

With his anger directed inward, Andrew feels depressed. He is fearful of the passage of time lest he have to surrender his fantasy of writing great fiction. His feeling of superiority toward his sister and his secretary because of their plain appearance may reveal his own inadequacy to appreciate subtler qualities in people; the pulp fiction he writes may be close to his own potential and he may be accepting the disproportionate amount of family obligation as a means of remaining on the creative level he is most comfortable with.

His relationship to his mother may make it difficult for him to forge close bonds with any other woman. He is the man of the household and does not have to form his own family unit to achieve this position. Still at an age when a third of his peers are as yet unmarried, it would nonetheless seem likely that the path of bachelorhood has been firmly laid for Andrew.

6

Marital Adjustment

However much courtship may have prepared the way for understanding and communication between the couple, adjustment efforts are generally necessary all through the years of marriage. New problems present themselves and must be coped with at various stages of married life.

In the early years of marriage, family planning is an important area of decision-making. "Moses Supposes" shows the college marriage facing the not uncommon difficulty of an unexpected pregnancy. With many of their adolescent tasks still unfinished, the two students must face the responsibilities of parenthood. Because of their affection for each other, their problems are more hopeful of solution than those of the childless couple in "Late in the Season." The latter story suggests that "communication," a popular concept in family life education, can serve marital adjustment only when the basic feelings of the couple are positive. In this story frankness would only reveal the deceit on which the marriage was founded.

"Faces of Hatred and of Love" reveals the therapeutic power of marital interaction, although the crisis of an infant's death soon reactivates all the old self-doubts. "This Morning, This Evening, So Soon" offers a more positive outcome, emphasizing the health-giving aspect of constructive family interaction. This story of interracial marriage offers even more illumination of parent-child relationships among minority groups.

In the early years of marriage patterns of dependency may be frustrating to the establishment of new relationships, as the mate may perceive attachment to the parental home as rejection of himself. "Mother to Dinner" provides a rather extreme example of the pull and tug of conjugal and filial loyalties. "Jack the Greatest" shows as a basic problem in teenage marriage the failure to have achieved independence from the family of origin. "Bitter Honeymoon" offers insights into early sexual adjustment, particularly in the context of divergent values. In "Revelation" the phenomenon of "running home to mother" after a quarrel is depicted, evidently an unconstructive solution in several cultures. "A Question of Blood" shows how child rearing brings a challenge to marital stability when neither mate will adjust to the expectations of the other. This story of interracial marriage contrasts with the harmonious resolution depicted in "This Morning, This Evening, So Soon." "The Star Blanket" examines the difficulties in marital adjustment when there are wide disparities of age and of interest. "Rope" reveals the thought processes of a husband and wife engaged in a domination struggle; their quarreling is unproductive and it is evident that repetition is inevitable. "My Oedipus Complex" shows the strain put on marital relationships when new parents have different conceptions of discipline, different tolerance thresholds for noise and disorder, different expectations of father and mother roles. Written with humor, the story nonetheless points up some of the serious conflicts between conjugal and parental behaviors which may persist until the nest has been emptied.

Growing apart can come early in the marriage, as in "Year of Grace" or later. The failure to develop joint interests and the consequent sense of loneliness on the part of one spouse find illumination in

"Two Bluebirds," "The Eighty-Yard Run," and "Marriage à la Mode." The first story shows the wife feeling shut out and superflous while the other two stories put the husband in the same uncomfortable position. The emotional distance between husband and wife may grow hopelessly wide if, as in "Uncle Wiggily in Connecticut," the wife lives with a fantasy image of a lost perfect love and keeps measuring her husband by this unreal yardstick. "At Mrs. Farrelly's" shows a wife whose needs are met in a marital relationship marked by the husband's alcoholism and work avoidance.

Problems of infidelity, whether real as in "Homage to Shakespeare" or feared as in "The Newlywed," "The Prophecy," and "The New Office Worker," are shown to be rooted in an impaired self-image or in uneven growth of the marriage partners. The latter, it is suggested in "The New Office Worker," is more amenable to improvement; an effort is made to retrieve a deteriorating marital situation by deliberately removing the temptation to adulterous involvement.

Further insights into the continuous process of marital adjustment can be gained from stories of aging and bereavement, the supreme tests of the sense of personal and social fulfillment.

"MOSES SUPPOSES"

Discussion Themes:

Changing roles of men and women
College marriages
Communication
Divorce
Dominance-submission
Mate selection
Pregnancy
Step-parents
Family-community relationships

Patrick, twenty, has followed his young bride Mona, eighteen, out to the deserted beach house of his mother-in-law. He is bewildered and depressed by Mona's sudden disappearance from their apartment near the college. When he finally gets Mona to talk, he is relieved to find that she cares for him. She had run away when, on learning she was pregnant, she had been overwhelmed by remembrances of her own childhood with a mother who made a succession of marriages. Her panic had been intensified by sudden awareness of the kind of world into which she was bringing a child, precipitated by a hostile remark of a passerby.

Patrick's offer to leave school and work full time to support his family is summarily rejected by Mona, who insists they will borrow against her inheritance instead. It is not clear whether Mona will have to surrender her educational goals. Nor is there any indication that either will take any responsibility for improving the "crummy world." However, beneath the despair and self-doubt, there is evidence that Mona and Patrick feel confident they will be able to offer their child more security than Mona had found in her childhood.

"LATE IN THE SEASON"

Discussion Themes:
Communication
Family planning
Quarreling: constructive and destructive
Mate selection

Cici and Frank Avery, both thirty, are now after a year of marriage constantly quarreling. On this day as they are driving toward the New England farm owned by Cici's father they are filled with resentment toward each other. Cici had married Frank because time was running out and she wanted children. Unaware of the priority of this motivation in her acceptance of him, Frank has been insisting that they put off having children for a while. Cici's jibes all tend to impugn Frank's manliness and have awakened in him anger and anxiety.

A huge turtle in the road offers an excuse for resumption of their quarrel. Cici insists on taking it into the car; Frank wants to kill it. She identifies with the turtle as "late in the season" too, while Frank sees in the turtle the embodiment of their dominance-submission struggle.

They project on to the Jone family, too, their feelings about themselves, for babies and pregnancies are a conspicuous feature of the caretaker's household. It is Cyrus Jone who completes the job of killing the turtle when Frank, by now unsteadied by drink, attempts to do so as an assertion of manhood, and fails. The incident intensifies Cici's contempt and Frank's self-doubt. Both, preoccupied with their own needs, are unable to give empathic consideration to each other's frame of reference.

7

Parent-Child and Sibling Relationships

Parents do not have the same feelings about all their children. Similarly, the children in a family may have widely different perceptions of their parents.

Back of the diversity of relationships lies the fact that the coming of children has different significance for different couples as well as for each of the parents. Not only does the individual's experience in his family of origin affect his conception of the parent role but the societal valuation of sex, family size, and physical attributes may affect his relationship to his offspring. The sex and ordinal position of the child may influence his perception of himself as accepted or rejected by his parents. In any case, the nuclear family of industrialized society tends to intensify parent-child and sibling interaction.

Many short stories reflect the confusions that arise in intergenerational relationships in a rapidly changing society. A few, such as "Twenty-one" and "Peace for Geretiello," point up the relatively rigid expectations in the traditional patriarchal family setting.

Perhaps because they are brief, most stories concentrate on a single phase of the life cycle. The significant connections between early and later parent-child relationships are more frequently suggested than made explicit. Stories that illuminate parent-child relationships either focus on parents and young children or older parents and grown children.

"My Oedipus Complex" and "The Downward Path to Wisdom" are of the young children category, although the latter story also offers some insight into adult sibling rivalry and the aging mother. "My Oedipus Complex" shows the young mother's problem in sharing her attention not only between her two children but among husband and children, and shows the need for marital cooperation in switching from dyadic to larger interaction. In "The Downward Path to Wisdom" the rejected child in a middle-class family has the hostilities among members of the older generation displaced onto him. In "Déjà Vu" the rejected child grows up to play a rejecting role toward her own children. Although the story tends to the melodramatic, it can stimulate discussion of the internalization of hated characteristics. In "Homage to Shakespeare" it is the father who is the rejecting parent.

"Charles" deals with a mother's reactions to reports of classroom misbehavior when she thinks her own child is not involved. It encourages examination of the concept of responsibility for children other than our own.

The father who cannot see his child reared in any image but his own is shown in "A Question of Blood."

In "We're All Guests" children of different ages and sex react diversely to the alcoholic father, the divorced mother, and the prospective stepfather, with the most negative effects on the adolescent boy. The vulnerability of the young adolescent is also shown in "The Bronco-Buster," "Who Lives Alas Away," "A Mountain Summer," "A Start in Life," and "Sherrel."

That the inevitable risk-taking in the rearing of children must sometimes end tragically is poignantly told in "The White Ribbons of the Curling Surf." In "War" the loss of the grown child is equally painful to the parents. "Holiday" deals with transformation of family relationships when illness brings the child permanent disability. The impact of the anti-social family member on parent and siblings is delineated in "Morning Sun."

The late adolescent or young adult is the product not only of diverse child-rearing attitudes and techniques characteristic of the various strata and subcultures, but of socializing agencies other than the family. Parents rarely see their children in these societal terms and often tend to blame themselves or reproach the child when his development is disappointing. The young adult, too, tends to self-blame or to recriminations. College students often have feelings of hostility and resentment toward family members. The stories give them an opportunity to recognize and give expression to some of these feelings through identification with the emotions of fictional youth who are similarly ambivalent toward relatives.

The stories also provide an opportunity to identify with the parents in some of the feelings experienced by the older generation as it tries to deal with its own confusions, disappointments, and feelings of inadequacy. The awareness that parents are "caused," that there have been determining influences in the shape of *their* parents and siblings and their life circumstances, not only encourages the development of some degree of understanding and compassion, but points up the problems the younger generation will have to solve in relation to their own future children.

One of these problems is self-determination in the realm of values. "My Little Boy" shows some of the positive aspects of parental influence on value formation in the early socialization process. In "Bridgeport Bus" and "Everything That Rises Must Converge," parents are affronted when their children develop values of their own.

In "Wife of the Hero" anticipation of such parental umbrage inhibits the establishment of a personal value system.

"Sunday Dinner in Brooklyn" shows not only the difficulty of communication when there is a wide educational gap between generations but reveals the anxiety and self-doubt of parents when their son seems to be rejecting their values. The theme has been well explored in nineteenth-century fiction, notably by Turgenev, but this short story provides insight into the problem of anomie, the modern form of nihilism that lacks the commitment to science and leaves the beatnik a critic without a platform. The story is also illuminating of the desperate loneliness of the empty-nested parent, particularly if the flight of offspring is interpreted as rejection.

Discontent of parents with children and children with parents permeates "A Drive in the Country," in which appreciation of parent behavior ultimately develops; "Professorio Collegio," which shows parents fostering and criticizing dependency; and "The Peacocks of Avignon," in which the young adult is able through compassion for her mother to free herself to live without a burden of hatred and shame. In "This Morning, This Evening, So Soon," the child's anger at the father who cannot protect him from society's injustices shows the threat that racial prejudice holds for adequate performance of the parental role. In "Moses Supposes" a daughter faces the insecurity built up in her by a mother's marital history. In "A Country Weekend" a daughter shakes off the neurotic dependency of her father. The pain inflicted by a mother's well-intentioned efforts to create an opportunity for upward mobility is central in "The Dressmaker's Daughter."

Exploitation of children to meet financial needs is shown in "Bridgeport Bus" and "Family Scene"; similar exploitation to meet emotional needs is shown in "The Lovely Lady" and "It's an Old Story," both dealing with the widow and her son, one on an upper-upper social level and one on a lower middle-class level. "Faces of Hatred and of Love" shows the deserted woman taking vengeance on her son, the subtlety of this phenomenon in a wealthy home contrasting with its manifestation among the disadvantaged, as in "The Bronco-Buster."

Sibling rivalry which persists into adulthood is the theme of "The Masculine Principle," "The Mad Lomasneys," and "My Sister's Marriage." In the first story, feelings of inferiority before her sisters affect a girl's ability to handle courtship relations. In the second, the choice of mate is determined more by hostility toward sisters than by feelings for the man. And in the third story, a widowed father's overattachment to one daughter, who escapes him through marriage, awakens in the neglected daughter a need to gain his attention, even, if necessary, by sacrificing her own potential as a woman.

"MY OEDIPUS COMPLEX"

Discussion Themes:

The absentee father
Child-rearing practices
The new baby
Parental and spousal roles
Sex education
Changing roles of men and women
Family alliances

With his father in the Army, Larry has seen little of him. He has enjoyed for the first five years of his life his mother's almost undivided attention. The father's return brings an abrupt change in status, and Larry resents this "stranger" who usurps his privileges. The father is too preoccupied with financial worries and getting a job to build up his relationship with his little son. However, the coming of a new baby changes the family alliances. As the father feels excluded, he turns to Larry to find consolation.

"THE DOWNWARD PATH TO WISDOM"

Discussion Themes:

Grandparents
Family aids : kindergarten
In-laws
The family servant
Quarreling : constructive and destructive
Sex education

Four-year-old Stephen hears his parents quarreling violently. Once more he is rushed by the maid to his grandmother's for a long visit. He does not find warmth and reassurance there, for although his grandmother initially shows some understanding of his needs, she is influenced by the hostility her unmarried son, David, displaces on to his sister's child.

Stephen's one affirmative experience has been a brief stay in a kindergarten near the grandmother's house. To shut out full perception of his hostile world, he has developed a surface dullness, but in the friendly school environment he dares to be normally alert. His mother's coming for him, highlighted by a bitter quarrel with her brother and her mother, ends the chance for school to play a supportive role. Stephen is left at the end with little more than recognition of his hatreds. As he is driven roughly home by his irate mother, he chants a little song, "I hate . . ."

8

Family Disorganization

The urban family, with its limited economic functions, is peculiarly vulnerable to dissolution when the bonds of affection begin to loosen. Sometimes the members may remain together physically, keeping intact the family shell even though it is emotionally hollow; at other times there may be separation, divorce, or desertion. In the latter instances the remaining members may form a fragmented family unit or may disperse completely, with children going to boarding schools or homes of relatives or being placed by outside agencies in foster homes, institutions, or adoptive homes. Death of a parent or long-term absence owing to hospitalization or imprisonment will often necessitate similar reorganization.

Stories help students see the similarities in homes that are emotionally broken and those that have placed on the unhappy situation the stamp of legal finality. There is no divorce in "A Country Weekend," but many features of alienation are present, including infidelity and depression. Similarly, in "Tell Me a Riddle" the resentments accumulated through long years of shared poverty reduce the togetherness of the empty nest to the dimensions of a boxing ring, with mutual hostilities finally finding expression. "Two Bluebirds" and "Marriage à la Mode" show the marital relationship drained of all emotional significance, leaving one mate in each instance feeling like an outsider rather than an integral member of a family unit.

Disharmony of objectives and role concepts leave little to the marital relationship in "Late in the Season," "The Star Blanket," and "Homage to Shakespeare." In "Uncle Wiggly in Connecticut" emphasis is placed on the negative consequences for the child in a home that has only formal cohesion.

Bitter reaction to desertion is the theme of "Faces of Hatred and of Love" and of "The Bronco-Buster." "A Glance in the Mirror" suggests that anger in such a situation is no more corroding than a bland acceptance that is tied to status symbols rather than to persons.

The effects on the children, as well as the marriage partners, of the decision to divorce are examined in "Love and Like," "We're All Guests," "Moses Supposes," and "A Red-Letter Day." In "The Sojourner" and "The Paper House," two divorced men are shown as emotionally insecure, the first one manifesting this through self-doubt and depression, the second through hostility toward all women. In "Babylon Revisited" the father tries painfully to overcome the obstacle of a vengeful sister-in-law in order to rebuild a family unit. In contrast, "Ixion" reveals a father who has grown completely indifferent to his children after divorce.

"No Pain Whatsoever" shows the formalization of relationships and diminution of the capacity to relate affectionately in the circumstances of hospitalization for a chronic disease. "Thoughts in the Dark" presents the ability to face up to serious physical impairment and to build the marital relationship on a new level. In "Counterclockwise," menopausal imbalance interacts with other negative factors, such as sibling rivalry and second-generation alienation, to fragment a large family. In "The Return" the husband is unable to permit restoration of the marital relationship with a wife who had left him but has come back.

"A Mountain Summer" calls into question the custom of relatives taking in orphaned children, showing the difficulty of forming an effective family unit without a backlog of affectional experiences together or without a matching of values and interests.

Remarriage of divorced men and women raises many problems of mate selection, of visiting rights where children are involved, and of relationships with former spouses and the children of prior marriages. In "The Sojourner" and "The Other Two," former husbands meet their successors. The latter suggests the emotional hazards that visiting privileges present for the adults. "Love and Like" adds the equally great hazards for the children themselves. "We're All Guests" reveals that the stepfather may be as differently perceived by the various children as was their father.

All the stories of divorce encourage examination of the personal and the societal dimensions of marital dissolution. They help the student arrive at an appreciation of the changing standards of satisfaction in spousal and parental roles and the great effort required to attain those standards. In a marriage preparation course these stories can sound a very sombre note. However, some of the anxiety they may arouse can be dispelled by efforts to locate the key factors in deterioration of the family relationships and to suggest points at which constructive action, including professional counseling, could have been taken.

"FACES OF HATRED AND OF LOVE"

Discussion Themes:

Bereavement: infancy
Communication
Desertion
Illness
Mate selection
The rejecting mother
Pregnancy

Paul, in his late twenties and tubercular, lives with his mother, Lady Foley, in her native France. When Paul was very young, his English father had deserted wife and child for another woman. The physical resemblance of Paul to his father facilitates the mother's displacement of hostility on to him. She needs Paul as this outlet and is able to use his illness to keep him at her side.

Paul plots to escape his mother's domination by wooing Simone, a girl so unattractive that his mother will not become suspicious. The plan succeeds, and the mother's anger when she realizes he has out-witted her brings to the surface the hatred she had not previously acknowledged. Overprotectiveness had been the cloak for her re-jection. She returns to England alone but does not long survive the loss of this love-hate relationship that had given her life some pur-pose.

Paul finds in Simone, unattractive, past hope for marriage, a com-parable prey to his own need to vent hostility. But the marriage brings him unexpected tenderness and peace, for Simone's gratitude and affection offer him the experience of an accepting mother. Preg-nancy, however, brings about a crisis their fragile union cannot with-stand. The doctor had advised Paul against marriage, urging instead entrance into a sanatorium. When the baby dies a few days after birth, Paul's feelings of guilt lead to depression and drink. When he recovers sufficiently to try to make up with her, Simone is hostile and retaliatory, her own feelings of inadequacy reactivated by the trying experience. She is unwilling to meet Paul's need to defend himself from recognition of his role in the baby's death, and bitterly tears down the curtain of denial he had erected.

The anger Paul now feels he displaces on to Simone; her response is a destructive assumption of the mother's earlier role of vengeful closeness. At the end they are living together, awaiting the death which was inescapable for him but which she has chosen for herself in order to be at hand to watch him die. With no pattern of open communication built up, Paul is unable to talk to Simone about the ambivalence he still feels, the love along with the hate, that could be the basis of a *rapprochement* to ease their torture of themselves and of each other.

"LOVE AND LIKE"

Discussion Themes:

Alimony
Children of divorce
Quarreling: constructive and destructive
Infidelity
Visiting rights
Mate selection: remarriage

Dan Shaper, divorced a month and now living in New York, has flown to Cleveland to see his two little girls, Paula, six, and Cynthia, four, who are living with their mother. He also visits Sally with whom he had had an affair in the final bitter year of a ten-year marriage.

Dan is incapable of taking up a life with Sally or with any other woman until he has resolved his feelings about his former wife. He envies her the home and the children and, above all, her feeling of being less at fault than he in their marital failure. Her neurotic preoccupation with the need for a male child, for which she had undergone expensive psychoanalytic therapy, was socially more acceptable than his own infidelity.

The visit is filled with strain: he must answer the difficult questions the children put to him and explain the difference between "like" and "love" in relationships between parents. Dan seeks to suppress his resentment toward his wife in order to preserve the memory of what had been good in his marriage. She feels a need to raze the entire past and be freed to rise, phoenixlike, to a new marriage. She insists, probably with punitive intent, on additional funds for private school fees for the children. When he resists, reminding her that he is now reduced to living in a single furnished room, she has an excuse to express her rage in a public quarrel and thereby further alienate the bewildered children from their father. His anger turns inward, leaving him prey to suicidal thoughts. It has become painfully clear to him that his wife will not help to relieve his guilt feelings by acknowledging any of her own contributions to the calamitous outcome.

"WE'RE ALL GUESTS"

Discussion Themes:

Alcoholism
Children of divorce
Adolescence
Mate selection: remarriage
Siblings
Visiting rights
Mother-son relationships

Chris is fourteen and Tory a year younger when their parents are divorced. The father, who had suffered war injuries, had begun to drink excessively. Tory and the younger brothers had been fond of him and had looked forward to his good-natured imaginative play. But the drinking bouts grew longer and he stayed away more often.

Only Chris among the children had reacted with hostility, for with reactivation during early adolescence of attachment to the mother, he had identified wholly with her in her anger.

While Chris becomes the man of the house and his mother uses him as confidant and companion to fend off her loneliness and depression, Tory daydreams about going off with her father and keeping house for him. This family romance is shattered when the father goes to a distant city and does not communicate with the children.

Tory's grief when Chris, resenting her affection for the father, fails to tell her of his coming, expresses itself in self-punishment and alerts the mother to the dangers involved. The mother shows less sensitivity in her relationship with Chris. With the arrival of Mr. Wagner, an old beau, her needs for adult companionship are met and she expects her adolescent son to resume a child role. She offers him little help in making the status change, possibly owing to feelings of guilt in her exploitation of him in the first months after the divorce.

Tory gradually develops an interest in the romantic figure about to enter the family. Chris, desperate to secure an ally against his rival, tries to make her regress to her sick longings by deceiving her about a gift from her father. But by this time she has developed sufficient strength to withstand his efforts, and Chris must face the inevitability of his mother's remarriage. In despair he gets drunk, thereby repeating an act of the rejected father, and tries vainly to get his siblings to share his sense of alienation from the parental home.

9

Aging
and the Aged

The longer life span of men and women in many modern societies has necessitated a shift in the signposts that mark the stages of the family cycle. The menopause and the onset of old age for women often coincided. Today the two may be separated by a gap of a decade or two, a gap expected to widen even further in the future. There is often a confusion in self-image, with men and women feeling young in their forties, fifties, and sixties, yet remembering that their parents at those ages had been considered old. The literature of earlier centuries sometimes deepens this confusion because the writers reflect the views of their day concerning the perilous dividing line of forty.

With longevity has come a societal as well as an individual problem of great significance for family relationships. Large numbers now face retirement who in previous generations would barely have survived the period of active family support. They are asked to play a role for which society offers little in the way of precedent. Some lessening of the problem would come from a reconsideration of the age of retirement. However, economic institutions in American society are not yet geared to continue the employment of older people who retain their work-performance capabilities for decades longer than before.

On the personal level, therefore, the threat of role discontinuity frequently confronts a man while he is still physically vigorous and eager to maintain his work life. A similar threat faces the woman if she has been working outside the home. For the homemaker, there is another role discontinuity which her grandmother did not have to cope with, namely, the conjugal emphasis after long years of child-rearing. A generation or two ago in the United States, parents did not long survive the marriage of the last of their offspring. Now with fewer children, arriving earlier and being married off sooner, the "empty nest" designates a common phenomenon, a home in which parents remain alone for some decades after their children have set up family units of their own, often far removed geographically.

Middle-aged parents have problems of relationship not only with adolescent children but with their own aging parents. Urbanization and the new emphasis on emotional satisfaction in family relationships have combined to upset the former expectancy, still operative in many other societies, that aging parents and their adult children will form a single household. City apartments are rarely adequate to meet the standards of privacy and comfort established for a large part of the population and sedulously cultivated by the mass media. Nor does the urban setting permit the contribution to the family economy that older folk are able to make on farms. Moreover, grown children who do not perceive their parents as having met their emotional needs in earlier years tend to be reluctant to play a nurturing role to newly dependent members of the older generation. And, unlike their counterparts in India, for example, who are eager to garner the rewards of age, elderly parents themselves are not always sure they wish to surrender the independence they have been taught to value.

The short stories illuminate many of these issues, permitting students to express the anxieties they feel concerning the aging of their own kin and encouraging an examination of the institutional changes that lie back of present contradictory expectations. Out of this can came clarification of the ethical dimension of relationships with the older generations and awareness of the possibility of restructuring social arrangements in keeping with the findings of gerontology.

"The Heyday of the Blood" can lead to a discussion of the mutual obligations of older and younger members of a household. "The Picnic" shows that these same questions arise even when the grandmother maintains her separate domicile. "Family Scene" and "The Gay Old Dog" exemplify problems of aging among the unmarried; in the latter story the need to blame others and the intensification of regrets increase with the passage of time. "Family Scene" suggests the envy felt by the aging for the easier existence of the younger generation. In "Peace for Geretiello" it becomes evident that the maintenance of the patriarchal role in old age is at great physical cost and is as negative in consequences as role reversal. Solutions, it becomes clear, must be sought between the polarities.

Old age is shown as intensifying problems already long in existence in a family's relationships. Thus, in "My Apples," the overindulgent mother as she ages interacts ever more destructively with her son. In "Tell Me a Riddle" the final years of a marriage bring out long suppressed resentment. This story encourages discussion of new alternatives in process of development for elderly men and women who do not want to join the households of their children or maintain their own, such as the homes for the aged that do not carry the opprobrium of older institutions in which the feeble and the indigent were hidden "over the hill." "Old Man Minick" explores this topic in the context of a solution found by an elderly widower for his loneliness in the home of a married son. This story contrasts with the melodramatic outcome of the frustration and rage that accompany the enforced togetherness of an old man and his daughter-in-law in "The White Rooster." Annoyance with even brief visits of an aged widower is depicted in "The Leader of the People."

While women tend to outlive men in American society, their household skills make it less mandatory that they join the family of their married children. This may explain the relative infrequency of stories dealing with the widowed mother in the household of a married son or daughter. The mass media more often publish stories on this theme, possibly reflecting the fears of their women readers rather than the actual problems now faced. However, in all media a frequent theme is the aging widow who tends to cling to an unmarried son or daughter. Examination of this problem is facilitated by "Bridgeport Bus," "Childybawn," "Everything That Rises Must Converge," "Faces of Hatred and of Love," and "Family Scene."

"The Prophecy" suggests some of the bases for infidelity in middle age: growing awareness of distance from professional or personal goals, projection on to a mate of anxiety about aging, and general lack of satisfaction in pattern of living.

"Clothe the Naked" depicts both the helplessness of the very old in the face of diminished employment opportunity and the emotional contribution they can still make to younger family members. In a more prosperous setting, as in "The Best Years," the aging tend to look back nostalgically to their years of struggle and of grief.

"Neighbor Rosicky" shows the difficulty, especially for the male, of adjusting to the change in work capacity brought on by advancing years and accompanying physical impairment. "The Light of the Sea," like "The Telegram," is concerned with the tendency to ignore the aged, to forget the pleasures once mutually enjoyed, but adds the dimension of retaliation open to the wealthy who have inheritances to bestow.

"A Sense of Tribe" is particularly provocative of discussion about the funeral as a family event. The different emotional investments of the dying and the kin are suggested in the old man's lamentation for the funerals of yesteryear when death focused the attention of the whole tribe on the one family member. Some of the negative effects are subtly revealed in his panegyric.

"THE HEYDAY OF THE BLOOD"

Discussion Themes:
Aging
Family life: rural
Rights and responsibilities
Risks and values
The extended family

Professor Joseph Mallory tells the story of his great-grandfather, Gran'ther Pendleton, who lived on the Mallory farm. At eighty-eight the old man took eight-year-old Joey to a fair in a neighboring town in Vermont. This was against the doctor's orders and against the wishes of Joey's parents. The old man did not consider it worthwhile to preserve his life at the cost of giving up the pleasures and adventures which gave it meaning for him. Nor, it is evident, did he consider himself under any obligation to reduce the amount of anxiety and labor he brought to relatives who had to nurse him after each such escapade.

Professor Mallory remembers warmly and proudly the model provided by the old man of parent-defying behavior and willingness to take risks. Perhaps unconscious hostility toward the middle generation facilitates the identification between the youngest and the oldest in this family.

"OLD MAN MINICK"

Discussion Themes:

Aging
Homes for the aged
In-law relationships
Peer groups: "senior citizens"
The widower

Pa Minick is left a widower after long years of married life. His income after retirement is adequate to support him but, unfamiliar with domestic chores, he is unable to maintain a separate household. Rather than leave a familiar city, he refuses his daughter's invitation and goes to live in his son's home nearby. His daughter-in-law Nettie, who has worked hard since early adolescence, seeks in marriage a vacation from responsibilities. She has put off having children and uses the presence of Pa Minick as a further excuse for delay. Overhearing this one day, he decides to take a step he had already been considering, that of entering an old men's home with his remaining income. Even with no open friction, Pa Minick had felt lonely and ill at ease. He particularly missed the companionship of his peers when bad weather shut him off from his park cronies. His insistence that Nettie have a child seems to have a threefold basis: he associates womanly kindliness, from which he himself had long benefited, with the mother role; as he grows older he is increasingly convinced that he knows what is best for everyone; and he has greater need for family perpetuation as death comes closer to him.

10

Bereavement

The loss of relatives, those dear and those not so dear, raises many problems for the survivors and constitutes one of the most profound challenges the family has to face. The personal reaction of each family member to bereavement reflects not only his fundamental beliefs but his pattern of need. The environmental circumstances of the loss often affects the kind of response. The stories show the many alternative ways of expressing grief and coping with the aftermath of bereavement.

The deleterious effects of the prolongation of grief are shown in "Who Lives Alas Away," when parents are preoccupied for a long time with their sorrow and their guilt feelings and fail to provide emotional support for their remaining child in her loneliness. In "Sherrel" a sibling's sense of guilt, deriving from the fantasy of the power of a death wish, is reinforced by the mother in her unconscious need to displace her anger on to the surviving child. Frequently in adolescence the feelings associated with an earlier bereavement experience are reactivated, and a resolution is sought.

The loss of a child brings guilt feelings to a mother who had permitted the child to risk a dangerous swim, in "The White Ribbons of the Curling Surf." The story also illustrates, as does "War," the defense against the possibly shattering effect of death by only gradual acceptance of it as a reality. In "Faces of Hatred and of Love" the infant's death reactivates earlier feelings of insecurity in the parents, creating a degree of self-blame that is destructive to their relationship. In "My Apples" the aging mother, bereaved of one son in the war, lavishes on the other a desperate overindulgence.

The loss of a mother leaves the orphan in the loving but aged hands of his grandmother in "Clothe the Naked." In "Déjà Vu" the loss of a mother leaves her children untouched, as her rejection of them has left them incapacitated for loving and caring.

In "Uncle Wiggily in Connecticut" the "halo effect" of bereavement prevents a realistic assessment of the deceased lover. "What the Cystoscope Said" shows two extremes of response to crisis: the son's self-punishing involvement in a father's last agonies and cremation contrasts with the escape into temporary illness unconsciously sought by the mother.

The loss of a family member may intensify the hopelessness of arriving at an improved level of interaction. In "Everything That Rises Must Converge," which offers one instance of this, the son's guilt feelings in his mother's sudden death also combine with anger because bereavement thwarts his dependency needs. Similarly, in "Tell Me a Riddle" the sense of loss is intensified by knowledge of the gulf still yawning between two family members, in this instance at the onset of a terminal illness.

"The Apple Tree" shows the mechanism of denial as a defense against guilt feelings; this is also one of the insights of "Peace for Geretiello."

The funeral can contribute to bringing the finality of death into

awareness, and community grief may as in "Holiday" facilitate re-
covery among the survivors. However, the participation of children
is a disputed matter. On the one hand, stress is placed on the possible
traumatic effects of such experiences; on the other, the danger of
making children feel rejected by excluding them from family interaction and confused by efforts at concealment around them. "A
Death in the Family" offers an extreme instance of the negative effects on a small boy when a mother alone attends the funeral of the
man she had hoped to marry; the child's fantasies of having killed the
unwelcome suitor by power of the death wish are reinforced. "A
Sense of Tribe" offers evidence on both sides of the issue of children's
participation in family activities concerned with bereavement.

"A Mountain Summer" reveals the contending needs and forces
operative in the aftermath of bereavement: the pathos of the orphaned child is presented along with the problems faced by those
who offer to become parent surrogates. The story also shows that
the abrupt severing of a sibling alliance may be interpreted by a child
as a kind of second bereavement.

"In the Middle of the Fields" suggests that the strong sense of loss
may continue into a second marriage. In this story the earlier and
the later phases of bereavement are depicted in the confrontation of
a new widow and an old widower. "The Other Two" indicates that
some of the same kinds of readjustment in relationships are required
in other kinds of separation as in bereavement.

The many stories that deal with widows and their grown children
show the role dislocations that occur in the fragmented family, with
sons or daughters being asked to fulfill economic and emotional responsibilities more characteristic of a marital partner. "It's an Old
Story," "Bridgeport Bus," "Family Scene," "Judas," "Everything
That Rises Must Converge," and "The Lovely Lady" place the
widow in the center of family disharmony. That separation or divorce may sometimes have bereavement effects is shown in the
stories of family disorganization, such as "Faces of Hatred and of
Love," "A Red-Letter Day," "The Sojourner," and "We're All
Guests."

"The Best Years" shows that a family can cope with its grief for
a beloved member and be sealed by their love for one another from
any traumatic effects. This is one of the very few stories that stresses
the positive rather than the problematical in a crisis that each family
inevitably experiences.

"A MOUNTAIN SUMMER"

Discussion Themes:

Adoption
Early adolescence
Family feuds
Orphans
Wills

Junius and Gillman live alone with their father, having lost their mother when they were very young. Now, when Junius is a sixth grader and Gillman in high school, their father dies too. Long ailing, he had never made a will. He had been for many years estranged from his parental home, and it is only at the funeral that the boys meet their relatives. The grandfather's hostility and resentment toward his son seem to be carried over to the grandchildren; he may be unconsciously blaming them for providing the emotional nourishment which had enabled his son to maintain the estrangement.

It is decided among the adults that the boys are to be sent to live with their father's half-sister, Aunt Hazel, and her husband, Lewis Wace, who have no children of their own.

The boys had always depended on each other for companionship. Even at home they had not made friends with other children, perhaps following the pattern of isolation set by their father. But they had been busy and useful, not only in farm chores, but in sharing their father's cultural pursuits. Their new home presents them with several challenges. Gillman, as a young adolescent, is consistently more threatened than the younger brother in the new situation. He is ready to take offense at any reminder that he is a dependent. Wace's warnings about scuffing the luggage or spending too much on clothes could be sore points for an adolescent even in a secure parent-child relationship. Moreover, the boys have too much idle time, for the driving lessons begun by Aunt Hazel have been stopped by her husband. A schoolyard fight by Gillman with the son of Wace's boss is assumed by Wace to have played some part in defeating his hopes for promotion and this intensifies the threat the adolescent boy represents for the middle-aged male. Aunt Hazel begins to identify with her husband in his resentment and agrees to send Gillman back to the rejecting grandfather. Gillman represses whatever feelings he has about being sent away from Junius but the younger boy suffers intensely from the forced separation, finding relief from his grief in this new loss by an open display of his anger toward the foster parents. Junius bids fair to outdo his brother in the various testings of authority which are usual in adolescence but which are much more difficult for both generations when a backlog of affection and mutual trust has not been built up.

"WHO LIVES ALAS AWAY"

Discussion Themes:

Adolescence
Dating
Family mobility: geographical
Siblings
Bereavement: sibling
Bereavement: children
Communication

The first summer after the death of her brother David in an auto accident finds Janey unable to accept the reality of bereavement. She had depended on David for companionship in his visits home from college, having found it difficult to establish new relationships with her own age group in the small town to which they had moved when she was twelve. Moreover, Janey as a young adolescent had found in David a romantic ideal.

The parents, in their continued mourning, neglect Janey. The father feels guilty in his son's death because he had granted permission for use of the car. He tends to displace some of the anger he feels on to Janey, an easy target for criticism in her characteristic adolescent behavior. The mother regresses into the unreality of love-story magazines. In her contacts with reality she expresses anxiety, as in her excessive concern over meal preparation.

Both the parents equate heterosexual dating with normality and are falsely relieved when Janey starts going with Bert. She is seeking only to escape the home atmosphere in which feelings of grief are hidden and denied, and no communication on the emotional level is permitted among the three survivors.

Bert tries to force Janey to accept the fact of David's death by revealing he knows her secret, that she goes to the cemetery at night to talk to David. Her panic in realizing that even this outlet is now closed to her results in a confused scheme to get away from the hated town, even at the price of a joyless sex relationship with Bert. When the frightened boy fails to show up for the bike trip to the city, Janey in self-punishment rides her bike to a crack-up. The knowledge that she had deliberately tried to harm herself shocks her parents into a more open expression of their feelings. Her self-alienation and the alienation from her parents come to an end with her acceptance at last of the changes life and death must inevitably bring.

APPENDICES

A

Bibliography

RELATED READINGS

Accent on Teaching, S. J. French, ed. New York: Harper, 1954.

Especially "The Case Method in Human Relations," by H. Gibson, and "The Thought Process of Students in Discussion," by B. S. Bloom.

The Adolescent through Fiction, N. Kiell. New York: International Universities, 1959.

Uses literature for illustration of psychological principles concerning adolescent behavior. Each principle is matched with an excerpt from a novel. While this leaves little for the student to do in searching out underlying motivation, it is helpful background reading for the teacher.

The Dynamics of Learning, N. Cantor. Buffalo; Henry Stewart, 1956.

A challenging presentation of the philosophy and the psychology of student-centered education. A learning process which helps students work through to their own answers serves the cause of democracy and of mental health, it is maintained, by "promotion of human capacity for self-development and self-realization."

A Handbook for Teachers, B. B. Cronkhite, ed. Cambridge, Mass.: Harvard University, 1951.

Especially "How Shall We Evaluate Teaching?" by G. Allport and "Education for Democracy," by W. B. Donham.

Literature as Exploration, L. Rosenblatt. Progressive Education Association. Commission on Human Relations. New York: D. Appleton-Century, 1938.

A landmark in the human relations approach to literature and the encouragement of interdisciplinary cooperation. Written primarily for literature teachers, however, it reveals the differences in their responsibility for exploring the various potentialities of literature, including the esthetic, and the concentration on the human relationships that is the responsibility of the teacher using literature in family study.

Literature for Individual Education, E. Raushenbush. New York: Columbia University Press, 1942.

85

Still useful in pointing up the ways in which literature can facilitate the teacher's performance of a guidance role. However, it will be evident to the teacher in the social sciences that the literature teacher's handling of a topic like family life includes several dimensions which are not germane for other disciplines, notably the effort to put the stories into an interrelated literary structure.

The Stereotype of the Single Woman in American Novels, D. Y. Deegan. New York: King's Crown Press, Columbia University, 1951.

Demonstrates the use of literature to document a social thesis and provides background reading in study of the unmarried adult.

STORY LISTINGS:

Short Story Index. New York: Wilson, 1953. *Supplement,* 1950-1954. New York: Wilson, 1956. *Supplement,* 1956-1958. New York: Wilson, 1960.

A fourth volume, to cover stories from 1959 to 1963, is expected to be published in 1965 at the latest, and possibly in 1964. The extensive story listings are by subject categories but no annotation of content is provided or indication of story length. It is particularly useful to the teacher seeking an alternative anthology for a story in a collection that has gone out of print. To determine whether a story listed in *Short Story Index* is in print currently, three sources are helpful: *Paperbound Books in Print* (New York: Bowker, annual) provides subject, author, and title indexes, with the latest volume superseding previous volumes. For books that are not paperbound, *Books in Print* (New York: Bowker, annual) and *Subject Guide to Books in Print* (New York: Bowker, annual) provide the title of the book, the name of the author or editor, the name of the publisher, and the price of the book. In the *Subject Guide,* under "Short Stories (Collections of Short Stories by Various Authors)," books are listed under sub-categories such as "Short Stories, American" and "Short Stories, French."

Book Review Digest, New York: Wilson, 1905 to date.

". . . devoted to the valuation of current literature," offers under the title of a particular volume of short stories a list of the stories to be found there; it does not provide for short stories, however, the same excellent subject and title index by which, under "Fiction," novels will be found listed according to family-oriented categories, such as "Brothers and Sisters," "Middle Age," and "Sex Problems."

Reader's Guide to Prose Fiction, compiled by E. Lenrow. New York: D. Appleton-Century, 1940.

Describes itself in terms of the 1,500 novels it lists but actually includes a brief section entitled "Short Stories," in which a few of the better-known collections are listed.

Reading Ladders for Human Relations (rev. ed.), Margaret Heaton and Helen B. Lewis. Washington, D.C.: American Council on Education, 1955.

Lists books according to level of reader maturity and has its main usefulness below the college level. However, for the teacher who wishes to use the short story in elementary and secondary schools, there is insufficient bibliographic aid offered, both in indication of theme and in annotation.

Mirror: On Seeing Yourself in Books, A. L. Porterfield. Fort Worth; Texas Christian University, Leo Potishman Foundation, 1957.

Is similarly of limited usefulness as it includes few short stories in its extensive listings of books on human relationships themes.

STORY ANTHOLOGIES:

Series:

The Best American Short Stories
New World Writing
Prize Stories: The O. Henry Awards

These anthologies appear periodically, usually on an annual basis, under a variety of editorships and auspices, as shown in the Master List of Stories, Appendix B of the present booklet. All are available in soft covers, inexpensive editions suitable for student use. Hard-cover editions are available for all but *New World Writing,* which is distinguished by its inclusion of stories by foreign writers.

Single Collections:

Among the anthologies that are compiled from time to time, at least three were designed specifically for classroom use.

Thicker Than Water, W. R. Wunsch and Edna Albers, eds. New York: D. Appleton-Century, 1939.

While several of the stories are dated or concerned with family problems that are not as pressing in the current decade as they were during the depression years, many of the others are moving and insightful and have been included in the Master List of Stories in Appendix B.

Sociology through Literature, L. A. Coser, ed. Englewood Cliffs, N.J.: Prentice-Hall, 1963.

Story excerpts, mainly from novels, are given for the topics usually included in introductory sociology textbooks. The section on the family is only one among sixteen, and is limited to twenty-two pages, more than half of which offer excerpts on the family of the orient. The book has additional potential, however, if the teacher is willing to undertake the work of cross-reference not done by the editor, namely, to search out in the other sections, such as socialization and race relations, the excerpts that are immediately germane to family study. The teacher will still have to weigh the usefulness of excerpts against complete stories in the illumination of family issues.

Psychology Through Literature, Carolyn Shrodes, et al., eds. New York: Oxford University, 1943.

Used by the senior editor in her English courses, this anthology includes short stories and excerpts from novels in sections headed "Emotional Conflicts," "The Psychoses," and the like. The brief section on "The Influence of the Family" offers only excerpts, although it recommends several short stories for further reading. A serious disadvantage for classroom discussion are the introductions provided for each of the stories and excerpts. By giving one interpretation, stated very firmly, of the psychodynamics of the characters' behaviors, the editors present the student with a completed problem : hypothesis, evidence, and all. Many teachers will prefer story collections that let the student struggle through to one or more interpretations which he can pool and sift in the classroom rather than those that encourage him to memorize the analysis of the expert.

B

Master List of Stories

Alphabetically Arranged by Story Title

1. "The Apple Tree," John Galsworthy, 62 pp.
   In *Great Modern Short Stories,* New York: Random House Modern Library, 1942.
2. "At Mrs. Farrelly's," Joseph Carroll, 11 pp.
   In *The Best American Short Stories 1953,* Martha Foley, ed. New York: Ballantine, 1953.
3. "Babylon Revisited," by F. Scott Fitzgerald, 23 pp:
   In *The Pocketbook of Modern American Short Stories,* Philip Van Doren Stern, ed. New York: Pocket Books, 1943.
4. "The Best of Everything," Richard Yates, 20 pp.
   In *Prize Stories 1956: The O. Henry Awards,* New York: Doubleday, 1956. Also in *Writing Fiction,* R. V. Cassill, New York, Pocket Books, 1963.
5. "The Best Years," Willa Cather, 35 pp.
   In *Five Stories,* Willa Cather. New York: Vintage, 1958.
6. "Bitter Honeymoon," Alberto Moravia, 27 pp.
   In *Great Italian Short Stories,* New York: Dell, 1959 (Translated from the Italian). Also in *Bitter Honeymoon and Other Stories,* Alberto Moravia. New York: Farrar, Straus and Cudahy, 1952.
7. "The Blind Man," D. H. Lawrence, 25 pp.
   In *Great English Short Stories,* Christopher Isherwood, ed. New York: Dell, 1957. Also in *The Indispensable D. H. Lawrence,* Diana Trilling, ed. New York: The Book Society, 1951.
8. "Bridgeport Bus," Maureen Howard, 11 pp.
   In *Prize Stories 1962: The O. Henry Awards,* Greenwich, Conn.: Fawcett, 1962. Also in *The Hudson Review,* Winter, 1960-1961.
9. "The Bronco-Buster," Peggy Bennett, 15 pp.
   In *New World Writing,* Third Mentor Selection, New York: New American Library, 1953.

10. "Charles," Shirley Jackson, 5 pp.
    In *Seventy-Five Short Masterpieces,* Roger Goodman, ed. New York,
    Bantam, 1961. Also in *The Lottery,* Shirley Jackson. New York: Farrar,
    Straus and Gudahy, 1948.

11. "Childybawn," Sean O'Faolain, 9 pp.
    In *New World Writing,* Fifth Mentor Selection. New York: New
    American Library, 1954.

12. "The Colleagues of Mr. Chips," Samuel Sandmel, 24 pp.
    In *The Best American Short Stories 1961,* Martha Foley and David
    Burnett, eds. New York: Ballantine, 1961.

13. "Clothe the Naked," Dorothy Parker, 8 pp.
    In *Twenty Grand Short Stories,* Ernestine Taggard, ed. New York:
    Bantam, 1947.

14. "Counterclockwise," Elisabeth Larsh Young, 22 pp.
    In *The Best American Short Stories 1960,* Martha Foley and David
    Burnett, eds. New York: Ballantine, 1960.

15. "A Country Weekend," Marvin Schiller, 18 pp.
    In *New World Writing,* Eleventh Mentor Selection. New York: New
    American Library, 1957.

16. "A Day's Wooing," Erskine Caldwell, 9 pp.
    In *The Pocket Book of Erskine Caldwell Stories,* selected by Henry
    Seidel Canby. New York: Pocket Books, 1947.

17. "A Death in the Family," Wingate Froscher, 12 pp.
    In *The Best American Short Stories 1953,* Martha Foley, ed. New York:
    Ballantine, 1953.

18. "Déjà Vu," Miriam McKenzie, 10 pp.
    In *The Best American Short Stories 1962,* Martha Foley and David
    Burnett, eds. New York: Ballantine, 1963. Also in *New World Writing,*
    No. 18. New York: Lippincott, 1962; and in *Prize Stories 1962: The
    O. Henry Awards.* Greenwich, Conn.: Fawcett, 1963.

19. "The Downward Path to Wisdom," Katherine Anne Porter, 20 pp.
    In *Thirteen Great Stories,* Daniel Talbot, ed. New York: Dell, 1955.
    Also in *The Leaning Tower and Other Stories,* Katherine Anne Porter,
    New York: Harcourt, Brace, 1939.

20. "The Dressmaker's Daughter," Guido Piovene, 10 pp.
    In *Great Italian Short Stories,* P. M. Passinetti, ed. New York: Dell,
    1959 (Translated from the Italian). Also in *New World Writing,* Seventh
    Mentor Selection. New York: New American Library, 1955.

21. "A Drive in the Country," Graham Greene, 15 pp.
    In *Nineteen Stories by Graham Greene.* New York: Bantam, 1949.

22. "Eighteenth Summer," Hallie Burnett, 12 pp.
    In *Firsts of the Famous,* Whit Burnett, ed. New York: Ballantine, 1962.

23. "The Eighty-Yard Run," Irwin Shaw, 15 pp.
    In *Short Story Masterpieces,* Robert Penn Warren and Albert Erskine,
    eds. New York: Dell, 1954.

24. "Eveline," James Joyce, 6 pp.
    In *The Indispensable James Joyce*. New York: The Book Society, 1949.

25. "Everything That Rises Must Converge," Flannery O'Connor, 14 pp.
    In *The Best American Short Stories 1962*, Martha Foley and David Burnett, eds. New York: Ballantine, 1962.

26. "Faces of Hatred and of Love," Jean-Baptiste Rossi, 47 pp.
    In *New World Writing*, First Mentor Selection. New York: New American Library, 1952. (Translated from the French.)

27. "The Fall of Candida," Charles G. Bell, 17 pp.
    In *New World Writing*, Fifteenth Mentor Selection. New York: New American Library, 1959.

28. "Family Scene," Anna Maria Ortese, 20 pp.
    In *New World Writing*, Fifth Mentor Selection, New York: New American Library, 1954. (Translated from the Italian.)

29. "The Gay Old Dog," Edna Ferber, 27 pp.
    In *Thicker Than Water*, W. R. Wunsch and Edna Albers, Eds. New York: D. Appleton-Century, 1939. Also in *Contemporary Short Stories*, K. A. Robinson, ed. Boston: Houghton Mifflin, 1924.

30. "A Glance in the Mirror," Harvey Swados, 14 pp.
    In *The Best American Short Stories 1960*, Martha Foley and David Burnett, eds. New York: Ballantine, 1960. Also in *Nights in the Gardens of Brooklyn*, Harvey Swados. Boston: Little, Brown, 1951.

31. "The Heyday of the Blood," Dorothy Canfield, 9 pp.
    In *A Harvest of Stories*, Dorothy Canfield, New York: Harcourt, Brace, n.d. Also in *Twenty Grand Short Stories*, Ernestine Taggard, ed., New York: Bantam, 1947; and in *Hillsboro People*, Dorothy Canfield Fisher.

32. "Holiday," Katherine Anne Porter, 26 pp.
    In *Prize Stories 1962: The O. Henry Awards*. Greenwich, Conn.: Fawcett, 1962. Also in *The Atlantic Monthly*, December, 1960.

33. "Homage to Shakespeare," John Cheever, 11 pp.
    In *Firsts of the Famous*, Whit Burnett, ed. New York: Ballantine, 1962. Also in *Story Magazine*, November, 1937.

34. "The Human Element," Somerset Maughan, 44 pp.
    In *The Somerset Maughan Pocket Book*. New York: Pocket Books, 1942.

35. "In the Middle of the Fields," Mary Lavin, 14 pp.
    In *The Best American Short Stories 1962*, Martha Foley and David Burnett, eds. New York: Ballantine, 1962.

36. "In the Zoo," Jean Stafford, 29 pp.
    In *Prize Stories 1955: The O. Henry Awards*. Garden City, N.Y.: Doubleday, 1955. Also in *Stories*, John Cheever et al, New York, Farrar, Straus and Cudahy, 1953; and in *Writing Fiction*, R. V. Cassill, New York: Pocket Books, 1963.

37. "It's an Old Story," Steve Goodman, 9 pp.
    In *Thicker Than Water*, W. R. Wunsch and Edna Albers, eds. New York: D. Appleton-Century, 1939.
38. "Ixion," Glendon Swarthout, 13 pp.
    In *New World Writing*, Thirteenth Mentor Selection. New York: New American Library, 1958.
39. "Jack the Greatest," James Ellison, 15 pp.
    In *New World Writing*, Twelfth Mentor Selection. New York: New American Library, 1957.
40. "Judas," Frank O'Connor, 11 pp.
    In *Stories by Frank O'Connor*. New York: Vintage, 1956.
41. "Late in the Season," Peter Matthiessen, 9 pp.
    In *New World Writing*, Third Mentor Selection. New York: New American Library, 1953.
42. "The Leader of the People," John Steinbeck, 16 pp.
    In *The Pocket Book of Modern American Short Stories*, Philip Van Doren Stern, ed. New York: Pocket Books, 1943. Also in *The Golden Argosy*, V. H. Cartmell and Charles Grayson, eds. New York: Bantam, 1956.
43. "The Light of the Sea," Frieda Arkin, 13 pp.
    In *The Best American Short Stories 1962*, Martha Foley and David Burnett, eds. New York: Ballantine, 1962.
44. "Love and Like," Herbert Gold, 32 pp.
    In *The Best American Short Stories 1959*, Martha Foley and David Burnett, eds. New York: Ballantine, 1959. Also in *Fiction of the Fifties*, Herbert Gold, ed. New York: Doubleday, Dolphin Books, 1959.
45. "The Lovely Lady," D. H. Lawrence, 23 pp.
    In *The Indispensable D. H. Lawrence*, Diana Trilling, ed. New York: The Book Society, 1951.
46. "The Mad Lomasneys," Frank O'Connor, 30 pp.
    In *Stories by Frank O'Connor*. New York: Vintage, 1956.
47. "The Magic Barrel," Bernard Malamud, 18 pp.
    In *Fiction of the Fifties*, Herbert Gold, ed. New York: Doubleday, Dolphin Books, 1959. Also in *The Magic Barrel*, Bernard Malamud. New York: Farrar, Straus and Cudahy, 1954.
48. "Main Currents in American Thought," Irwin Shaw, 11 pp.
    In *Fifty Great Short Stories*, Milton Crane, ed. New York: Bantam, 1952.
49. "Marriage à la Mode," Katherine Mansfield, 13 pp.
    In *Great English Short Stories*, Christopher Isherwood, ed. New York: Dell, 1957. Also in *Short Story Masterpieces*, Robert Penn Warren and Albert Erskine, eds. New York: Dell, 1954.
50. "The Masculine Principle," Frank O'Connor, 24 pp.
    Stories by Frank O'Connor, New York: Vintage, 1956.

51. "Morning Sun," Mary Deasy, 12 pp.
   The Best American Short Stories 1953, Martha Foley, ed. New York: Ballantine, 1953.
52. "Moses Supposes," Ellen Currie, 19 pp.
   In *New World Writing*, Fourteenth Mentor Selection. New York: New American Library, 1958.
53. "Mother to Dinner," Tess Schlesinger, 22 pp.
   In *Thicker Than Water*, W. R. Wunsch and Edna Albers, eds. New York: D. Appleton-Century, 1939.
54. "A Mountain Summer," James Ballard, 25 pp.
   In *The Best American Short Stories 1953*, Martha Foley, ed. New York: Ballantine, 1953.
55. "My Apples," Robert Granat, 19 pp.
   In *New World Writing*, Tenth Mentor Selection. New York: New American Library, 1956.
56. "My Little Boy," Carl Ewald, 38 pp.
   In *World's Great Short Stories*. New York: World Publishing, 1942 (Translated from the Danish).
57. "My Oedipus Complex," Frank O'Connor, 13 pp.
   In *Stories by Frank O'Connor*. New York: Vintage, 1956. Also in *Short Story Masterpieces*, Robert Penn Warren and Albert Erskine, eds. New York: Dell, 1954.
58. "My Sister's Marriage," Cynthia Marshall, 13 pp.
   In *Prize Stories 1957: The O. Henry Awards*. Garden City, N.Y.: Doubleday, 1957. Also in *Mid-Century*, Orville Prescott, ed. New York: Pocket Books, 1958.
59. "Neighbor Rosicky," Willa Cather, 39 pp.
   In *Five Stories*, Willa Cather. New York: Vintage, 1958.
60. "A New England Nun," Mary E. Wilkins (Freeman), 11 pp.
   In *Anthology of Famous American Stories*. New York: Modern Library, 1953.
61. "The Newlywed," Yury Nagibin, 15 pp.
   In *Soviet Short Stories*, Avrahm Yarmolinsky, ed. New York: Doubleday, Anchor Books, 1960.
62. "The New Office Worker," Sergey Antonov, 15 pp.
   In *Soviet Short Stories*, Avrahm Yarmolinsky, ed. New York: Doubleday, Anchor Books, 1960.
63. "News for the Church," Frank O'Connor, 10 pp.
   In *Stories by Frank O'Connor*. New York: Vintage, 1956.
64. "None Sing So Wildly," James Jones, 33 pp.
   In *New World Writing*, Second Mentor Selection. New York: New American Library, 1952.
65. "No Pain Whatsoever," Richard Yates, 11 pp.
   In *Eleven Kinds of Loneliness*, Richard Yates, Boston: Little, Brown, 1957.

66. "Old Man Minick," Edna Ferber, 17 pp.
    In *Gigolo*, Edna Ferber, New York: Doubleday, 1922. Also in *The Golden Argosy*, V. H. Cartmell and Charles Grayson, eds. New York: Bantam, 1956.
67. "The Other Two," Edith Wharton, 23 pp.
    In *Fifty Great Short Stories*, Milton Crane, ed. New York: Bantam, 1959.
68. "The Paper House," Norman Mailer, 13 pp.
    In *New World Writing*, Second Mentor Selection. New York: New American Library, 1952.
69. "Peace for Geretiello," Luigi Forni, 11 pp.
    In *New World Writing*, Tenth Mentor Selection. New York: New American Library, 1956 (Translated from the Italian).
70. "The Peacocks of Avignon," Harvey Swados, 9 pp.
    In *Nights in the Gardens of Brooklyn*, Harvey Swados. Boston: Little, Brown, 1960.
71. "The Picnic," Christine Clegg, 17 pp.
    In *New Campus Writing No. 2*, Nolan Miller, ed. New York: Bantam, 1957.
72. "Professorio Collegio," David Shaber, 13 pp.
    In *Prize Stories 1962: The O. Henry Awards*. Greenwich, Conn.: Fawcett, 1962.
73. "The Prophecy," Arthur Miller, 36 pp.
    In *The Best American Short Stories 1962*, Martha Foley and David Burnett, eds. New York: Ballantine, 1963.
74. "A Question of Blood," Ernest Haycox, 4 pp.
    In *Seventy-Five Short Masterpieces*, Roger Goodman, ed. New York: Bantam, 1961. Also in *By Rope and Lead*, Ernest Haycox. Boston: Little, Brown, 1937.
75. "A Red-Letter Day," Elizabeth Taylor, 10 pp.
    In *Short Story Masterpieces*, Robert Penn Warren and Albert Erskine, eds. New York: Dell, 1954.
76. "*The Return*," Joseph Conrad, 68 pp.
    In *Tales of Unrest*, Joseph Conrad. New York: Doubleday, Page, 1923.
77. "Revelation," Rhys Davies, 10 pp.
    In *Sensual Love*, Don Congdon, ed. New York: Ballantine, 1959.
78. "Rope," Katherine Anne Porter, 6 pp.
    In *Twenty Grand Short Stories*. Ernestine Taggard, ed. New York: Bantam, 1947. Also in *Flowering Judas and Other Stories*, Katherine Anne Porter. New York: Harcourt, Brace, 1930.
79. "Saul," Michael Mason, 4 pp.
    In *New Campus Writing No. 2*, Nolan Miller, ed. New York: Bantam, 1957.
80. "A Sense of Tribe," Sarellen M. Wuest, 6 pp.
    In *New Campus Writing No. 2*, Nolan Miller, ed. New York: Bantam, 1957.

81. "Sherrel," Whit Burnett, 9 pp.
    In *The Best Short Stories 1932,* E. J. O'Brien, ed. Boston: Houghton, Mifflin, 1932. Also in *Thicker Than Water,* W. R. Wunsch and Edna Albers, eds. New York: D. Appleton-Century, 1939.
82. "The Sojourner," Carson McCullers, 10 pp.
    In *Short Story Masterpieces,* Robert Penn Warren and Albert Erskine, eds. New York: Dell, 1954. Also in *The Ballad of the Sad Cafe and Other Stories,* Carson McCullers. New York: Bantam, 1958.
83. "The Star Blanket," Shirley Schoonover, 20 pp.
    In *Prize Stories 1962: The O. Henry Awards.* Greenwich, Conn.: Fawcett, 1962. Also in *The Transatlantic Review,* Spring, 1961.
84. "A Start in Life," Ruth Suckow, 14 pp.
    In *Twenty Grand Short Stories,* Ernestine Taggard, ed. New York: Bantam, 1947.
85. "Sunday Dinner in Brooklyn," Anatole Broyard, 15 pp.
    In *Avon Book of Modern Writing No. 2,* William Phillips and Philip Rahv, eds. New York: Avon, 1954.
86. "The Telegram," Konstantin Paustovsky, 11 pp.
    In *Soviet Short Stories,* Avrahm Yarmolinsky, ed. Garden City, New York: Doubleday, Anchor Books, 1960.
87. "Tell Me a Riddle," Tillie Olsen, 33 pp.
    In *The Best American Short Stories 1961,* Martha Foley and David Burnett, eds. New York: Ballantine, 1961.
88. "That Lovely Green Boat," William Berge, 24 pp.
    In *Writing Fiction,* R. V. Cassill. New York: Pocket Books, 1962.
89. "This Morning, This Evening, So Soon," James Baldwin, 37 pp.
    In *The Best American Short Stories 1961.* New York: New American Library, 1961.
90. "Thoughts in the Dark," Tatsuzo Ishikawa, 4 pp.
    In *New World Writing,* Fourth Mentor Selection. New York: New American Library, 1953. (Translated from the Japanese.)
91. "Truth and Consequences," Brendan Gill, 4 pp.
    In *Seventy-five Short Masterpieces,* Roger Goodman, ed. New York: Bantam, 1961. Also in *The New Yorker* Magazine, 1941.
92. "Twenty-one," Tarjei Vesaas, 12 pp.
    In *New World Writing,* Fourteenth Mentor Selection. New York: New American Library, 1958. (Translated from the Norwegian.)
93. "Two Bluebirds," D. H. Lawrence, 18 pp.
    In *The Indispensable D. H. Lawrence,* Diana Trilling, ed. New York: The Book Society, 1951.
94. "Uncle Wiggily in Connecticut," J. D. Salinger, 16 pp.
    In *Nine Stories,* J. D. Salinger. New York: New American Library, Signet, 1954. Also in *Short Story Masterpieces,* Robert Penn Warren and Albert Erskine, eds. New York: Dell, 1954.
95. "War," Luigi Pirandello, 5 pp.
    In *Great Italian Short Stories,* P. M. Pasinetti, ed. New York: Dell,

1959 (Translated from the Italian). Also in *The Medals and Other Stories*, Luigi Pirandello. New York: Dutton, 1939.

96. "A Week of Roses," Donald Wesely, 10 pp.
    In *The Best American Short Stories 1953*, Martha Foley, ed. New York: Ballantine, 1953.

97. "We're All Guests," George R. Clay, 31 pp.
    In *New World Writing*, Eighth Mentor Selection, New York: New American Library, 1955.

98. "What the Cystoscope Said," Anatole Broyard, 30 pp.
    In *Fiction of the Fifties*, Herbert Gold, ed. New York: Doubleday, Dolphin Books, 1959.

99. "The White Ribbons of the Curling Surf," Mihal Rey, 8 pp.
    In *New Campus Writing No. 2*, Nolan Miller, ed. New York: Bantam, 1957.

100. "The White Rooster," William Goyen, 14 pp.
    In *Thirteen Great Stories*, Daniel Talbot, ed. New York: Dell, 1955.

101. "Who Lives Alas Away," Clare McGrath Butler, 25 pp.
    In *New World Writing*, Fifth Mentor Selection. New York: New American Library, 1954.

102. "Wife of the Hero," Sally Benson, 12 pp.
    In *Thicker Than Water*, W. R. Wunsch and Edna Albers, eds. New York: D. Appleton-Century, 1939.

103. "Winter Term," Sallie Bingham, 10 pp.
    In *The Best American Short Stories 1959*, Martha Foley and David Burnett, eds. New York: Ballantine, 1959.

104. "Year of Grace," Harvey Swados, 16 pp
    In *Nights in the Gardens of Brooklyn*. Boston: Little, Brown, 1960.

C

Index of Problem Areas
Covered in the Stories

Note: The numbers following the entries refer to the stories in the Master List of Stories, *not* to the page numbers.

 *bureau of publications*
teachers college
columbia university